Roy Benford's Journey

How To Navigate Detours, Adapt, Recover, And Stay Committed When Life Throws You Curveballs

Roy Lee Benford

This book is dedicated to my sons Malcolm Patrick and Marcel, and my grandsons Malcolm Jamal, Amani, Broaden, and Dahmion.

And to Julia McCray Johnson, the oldest family member on my mother's side of our family, who will turn 98 on her next birthday in December 2025.

About the Author

Roy Benford is an award-winning real estate broker and a Canfield Certified Trainer & Coach serving Oakland and the San Francisco Bay Area for more than 30 years. His passion and dedication for making the American dream a reality for his clients is why he ranked among the top 10 percent of over 11,000 Realtors in the Northern California/Hawaii Region.

His experience as a guest lecturer on college campuses and teaching classes for pre-licensees in private real estate schools is a testament to his commitment to helping others pursue their purpose. He is a member of the Allen Temple Baptist Church in Oakland, California, where he serves on the Public Ministry Committee. He is the past president of the Oakland Coalition of Congregations and a former board member of Education For Change, a partner charter operator to the Oakland Unified School District.

Roy achieved the rank of SPC 5 while serving in the U.S.

Army and was awarded the Bronze Star Medal for Meritorious Service while serving in Vietnam.

Roy currently lives in Oakland, California, near his two sons and four dynamic grandsons. On his days off, he and his family enjoy hiking, fishing, cooking, attending concerts, and local sporting events.

Contents

Introduction

Whatever you can do, or dream you can do, begin it. Boldness has genius, power, and magic in it. Begin it now.

— Johann Wolfgang Von Goethe

I stopped procrastinating and committed to writing this book after a chance encounter with a stranger in a hotel lobby in San Francisco. One summer night in 2019, I was seated at the bar in the lobby of the W Hotel in downtown San Francisco, waiting for a colleague, when I noticed two casually dressed young men who looked to be in their late thirties enter the lobby about 12 yards away. The lobby was packed with people. There was standing room only from the entrance to where I was sitting with my back to the bar, wedged between a couple on my left and a woman on my right.

The couple and I were facing away from the bar. As the young men worked their way through the packed lobby, in tandem, moving toward me at a slight angle from left to right, the one leading would look up at me every few yards. This continued until they were even with me. The leader stopped within 30 inches, give or take an inch, in front of me, turned his head slightly to his right, and without making eye contact, proceeded to peruse my face for about 15 seconds. He looked at my face as if he were looking at a painting.

He said, "You have a very interesting face." After pausing for several seconds, he continued, "You've seen some things," nodding his head slowly and ever so slightly, as if to confirm his observation.

During this encounter, I didn't flinch or say a word. I just looked at him looking at me. Then the men moved on, just as they had entered, pressing their way through the crowded lobby. I sat there, relieved, and reflected on what had just happened. The young man's words resonated with me then and now.

On November 14, 2022, while looking down at the Oakland Airport Traffic Control Tower in the distance from the picture window of my upstairs home office, I wrote the outline for the book you are now holding in your hands. This book is about my journey growing up in a small town in Texas, becoming an award-winning real estate agent and broker in the San Francisco Bay Area, and using that experience to become a Canfield Certified Trainer and Coach. At times, it is almost a stream of consciousness. You will find that I move from thought to thought quickly, seemingly at random. However, there is a method to my madness. My goal is to share my thoughts and perspective with you in a way that simulates how I, too, had those notions.

By the time the COVID-19 pandemic disrupted life as we know it and upset the residential real estate market, I had already begun using the knowledge and experience I'd accumulated over the past two and a half decades to expand my business into real estate education.

Shortly after I accepted a part-time instructor position with a private real estate school in San Pablo, California, an additional opportunity presented itself. I received a call from Guy Forkner, co-chair of the real estate department at Merritt College in Oakland, California. Mr. Forkner had viewed my profile on LinkedIn. He invited me to become a guest lecturer for his Real Estate Practice class of approximately 60 students. I considered the invitation an honor because Mr. Forkner was the co-chair of Merritt's Real Estate Department. His students were happy and excited to have me. They asked a host of very relevant questions and learned a lot from my answers.

The last line in Mr. Forkner's introduction of me to the class was, "Roy is a survivor." This line provided a good segue for me to lecture about the tough challenges agents have to overcome, the liability and the risks involved in each real estate transaction, and what agents must do to survive and thrive in the current market.

I enjoyed lecturing at Merritt. I even received a referral for a listing from one of the students whose mother wanted to sell her house. I was super excited when Mr. Forkner invited me back to lecture another class the following semester. Little did I know that I was going to have to pull out all my survival skills for what was to come next.

But first, let me share my beginnings. My journey started with me growing up on our family farm, working side by side with my dad in the dusty cotton fields in the Brazos Valley of Washington County, Texas. My activities on the farm included a plethora of chores, some of which made necessary contributions to our family's survival and quality of life. In this book, you will learn about my experiences, including walking three miles to and from elementary school, doing homework by lamplight, graduating from high school in the top 20 percent of my class, and being accepted into Prairie View A&M University. This is a testament to my faith, grit, and determination to succeed. I'm sharing this overview of my accomplishments in hopes that by doing so, you will be able to achieve similar and even greater success.

In some areas of this book, I paint my story with a broad brush. In other places, I go deeper into details like picking cotton with Papa Les, coaching little league baseball, describing the details of a real estate transaction, or volunteering with the American Red Cross. I drill down in the areas that support the main objectives of the book, which are to communicate how I have never allowed my current circumstances to dictate my future, and how I've met and overcome challenges of limiting beliefs, self-doubt, and negative self-talk.

I've built my business on the traits of authenticity, honesty, integrity, and vulnerability — qualities that build trust and strengthen relationships. Multiple client testimonials bear me out on this. I want you to know this truth:

Every individual whom you see as very successful operates on a set of success principles. They either have a coach now or have had one in the past.

Additionally, in this book, I describe how my years of experience and training by some of the brightest minds in the personal development field led me to the founding of my own coaching business. I coach others not only to be successful, but to find significance and fulfillment as a byproduct of success.

Although I have an extensive background in real estate, my coaching is not limited to real estate. The proven system I use for training is based on Jack Canfield's book, *The Success Principles*. My training and coaching apply to everyday individuals, athletes, executives, entrepreneurs, teachers, and coaches who want to gain greater self-awareness and achieve peak performance in their personal and professional lives.

I write in detail about the real estate market, including my knowledge and experience as a real estate professional, sharing how I've survived the ups and downs of the real estate market over the last 30-plus years. I also tell stories about listing and selling real estate, challenging transactions, and how I resolved issues as clues to how you may find solutions to the problems you encounter while pursuing your "BIG WHY." Further, I share my experience with being coached. I explain how coaching catapulted my real estate career by helping me increase my production to the top ten percent of over

11,000 sales associates in my region, Northern California, and Hawaii.

I share all of these experiences because I'm a product of my environment. This is what has made me who I am today. I share my values, knowledge, and experiences with you fully in this book in the hope that they not only resonate with you and others searching for clues to success, but also create a visible and rich path for you to follow.

During my career, I've had the privilege of being coached and trained by some of the brightest and most contemporary leaders in the field of personal development, namely Jack Canfield, Tom Ziglar, Lisa Nichols, Gary Keller, Tina Jones, Craig Proctor, Tim and Julie Harris of Harris Coaching, Nate Brooks, Sr., Patrice Washington, and Melinda Cohan, to name some of them. These leaders have been instrumental to my success. A National Association of Realtors Member Profile in 2021 revealed that seventy-five percent of new agents drop out of the business within the first year. It is also documented that after five years, eighty-seven percent of agents have left the business.

Now I coach others how to survive and thrive in all types of markets: the good, the bad and the ugly, and how to face and overcome the tough new challenges agents experience today. These include rapidly changing demographics, economic uncertainty, skyrocketing prices, the increasing use of real estate technology(such as digital platforms and Artificial Intelligence), and how to meet the expectations of highly knowledgeable, tech-savvy buyers and sellers. I sincerely believe that if you can learn anything from my experiences expressed in this book, you will be ahead of the game regardless of your profession or occupation. *Success leaves clues.*

Chapter 1
Core Values

Keep your values positive because your values become your destiny.

— Albert Einstein

I n my first year of elementary school, I did my homework by the light of a kerosene lamp. (I still have one on my desk, but I don't use it. It's been in the family for decades.) When the light grew dim, my dad would take a piece of newspaper and clean the globe of the lamp. The whole room would light up, and I could see clearly and complete my homework. In 1950, the Lower Colorado River Authority brought electricity to the rural areas, including our house.

Another memory I have is repairing our fence where the cows had pushed through the barbed wire and escaped to the nearby corn or watermelon patch. I would mend the fence, but then, frustratingly, the cows would get out the next day, or even sometimes the same day. One day, after my brothers and I had rounded up the cows once again and after we fixed the fence, we returned home to experience one of my dad's powerful teaching moments. We began by trying to explain how these constant cow escapes were continuously happening. I remember my dad posing the following question:

"Do you mean to tell me that the cows are smarter than you?"

Cows escaping from the pasture were a rare occurrence after that teaching moment.

CORE VALUES WERE INSTILLED EARLY ON IN MY LIFE

Living by my values has allowed me to be my authentic self in all areas of my life. My values have also caused me to pursue my life purpose with conviction and passion.

Every weekday morning, my parents huddled around the old brown Zenith radio and listened intently to the news and weather through the static fading in and out over the newscaster's voice. First, we listened to the local news. Then my dad would tune the radio to a station in Austin, Texas. Here, we got a broader view of what was happening at the state level, including all of the political news and the weather forecast for Austin and the surrounding areas. On Sunday mornings, before we went to church, there was preaching and singing on the radio.

My dad always reminded my siblings and me that we could be anything we wanted to be. When I was growing up, my dad taught me the value of hard work, honesty, truthfulness, service to others, and kindness; to always stand for what is right, to help those less fortunate, to stand by my word, and finally, to fight *for* my brothers and sisters, not *with* them.

We were instilled with the idea that "If one of you has something, all of you have something." He taught by word and deed. He was not big on saying, "I love you," but he always found ways to show it. He often reminded us, "Actions speak louder than words."

My parents also taught me these principles and proverbs: Do unto others as you would have them do unto you. You reap what you sow. Respect your elders. Pay your debts. Guard your reputation. Trust in the Lord with all your heart, and lean not on your understanding. Love one another. Every tub must sit on its own bottom. Honor thy father and thy mother (the fifth Commandment). He who buys what he does not need will often need what he cannot buy.

My dad was known for sharing wisdom and knowledge that he knew would last us a lifetime. One afternoon, while walking through the pasture on our way to repair a section of fence where the cows had broken through, my dad told me that there would come a time when I would want his advice, but he would not be there. He told me, "When that day comes and you want to know what my advice to you would be, pick up your Bible and go to the book of Proverbs, because what it says there is what I would tell you."

BORN TO LEAD: LEADERS CREATE LEADERS

As the firstborn of 4 boys and one girl, I was born to lead. My parents followed the doctrine of Proverbs 22:6: "Train a child up in the way he (or she) should go, and when he is old, he will not depart from it." By the age of four, I could recite the alphabet, read, and write my name. My early lessons came from studying the letters and numbers of the manufacturer's information on the wood-burning stove that was used to heat my parents' bedroom, which we treated as our family room.

By the time I could read and write well, I learned that the colorful papers with handwriting on them in the dresser drawer were Poll Tax receipts. These showed my dad's payments of poll taxes for himself and others in the community who couldn't afford to pay. The Poll Tax was enacted in 1889. The tax disenfranchised many blacks and poor whites. Jim Crow laws were implemented to enforce racial segregation in the South between 1877, the end of Reconstruction, and the late 1950s. On February 9, 1966, a federal court in Texas ruled that the state's poll tax was unconstitutional.

FAMILY GATHERINGS AT GRANDMA'S HOUSE

For as far back as I can remember, there was always a feast at my grandmother's house on Sundays and holidays. After church, we would climb into the family car — a beige 1949 Ford four-door sedan — and my dad would drive the five miles to her house. My three brothers and I would ride in the back, while my sister, Madelyn, rode in the front, sitting between my mom and dad. My aunts and uncles would already be there, having arrived from Houston around 10:30 A.M. with food items to complement the scrumptious meal my grandmother was preparing.

Auntie Hallie always brought one of her famous lemon meringue pies! During the Christmas season, they brought gifts for my siblings and me. We all sat on the front porch while the final touches of dinner were being prepared by my grandmother, Nicie Malone, and listened to the uncles tell some of the funniest stories you'd ever want to hear. My uncle George was the philosopher. One of his favorite sayings was, "It's a mighty poor rat that has but one hole!"

Uncle George and my dad enjoyed discussing the Bible. They would talk politics and religion until they exhausted whatever subject they happened to be on, sometimes agreeing to disagree.

MY FIRST DAY IN ELEMENTARY SCHOOL WAS UNFORGETTABLE

My dad drove me to Uncle Tom Benford's house, which was directly across the road from the school. He dropped me off early that morning before school opened so he could get back to the cotton fields and start working before 8:00 AM.

My cousin Pete, who was five years older than I, lived with his dad, Tom, also known as Little Tom, and his mother, Addie Belle. When we heard the school bell ring, we walked over, and I entered the school for the first time, marking the beginning of my elementary school education. After school, I would walk home with the other kids.

After the first few days of orientation, I walked to school every day, three miles each way, along with the neighbors' kids, who formed a group of eight or nine students. Sometimes, when it was cold and raining, one of the parents would drive us. I'll never forget my first day at school. My dad had provided me with a fresh haircut, leaving me practically bald on the sides and back. My hairstyle didn't sit well with the two bullies. One of them picked on me most of the day.

At the last recess of the day, they promised, "We're going to get you after school." On the way home, one of the bullies would run up behind me and thump me on the back of my head, then run up the road laughing as if to impress the other bully. He'd wait for me to catch up. When I'd pass him, he would run up behind me and thump the back of my head again. The other bully would laugh and tease me. This went on again and again.

Not wanting to make trouble on my first day of school, I fumed the rest of the way home. When my dad got home that evening, he wanted to know how my first day of school was. After sharing my best experiences from my first day, I then recounted what had happened to me on my walk home.

My dad knew the bullies' parents, so I was expecting him to deal with the issue parent-to-parent. That wasn't the case. My dad's response completely caught me off guard. He said, "That's your head. It's up to you whether or not you're going to allow somebody to thump it." That was the first and last day that this boy thumped my head. On our way home from my second day, I fought him until he broke and ran away. I never had to fight him again.

My first teacher was Mrs. Millie Lyons. On the first day of school, I was issued a pre-primer book entitled "We Come And Go." I can still see the little, colorful paperback book with a little white boy and girl on the cover, accompanied by their parents. It was a story about family life, where families moved to a new neighborhood, met new people, and later moved again, with a new family moving in. Thus, "we come and go."

By the second week of school, I had read the little paperback pre-primer book from cover to cover twice. The next week, she gave me the primer, and I finished that book in one week. After that, I was bored and read everything with writing on it, including advertising, highway signs, and even Burma Shave and cigarette packages. Sears & Roebuck and Montgomery Ward's catalogs were not safe, either. I love to read to this day.

Mrs. Maggie Simpson was my fourth-grade teacher. She was more than a teacher and a principal. She was a mentor. She taught me so much more than I could have learned from books alone. When I finished the books she issued me, she would open the bookroom and let me go in to choose whatever book I wanted to read. When it was my time to read, she'd call me up and I'd read whatever book I'd chosen. She would bring the Houston Post newspaper to school every day, which I would read between my class assignments. I conducted science experiments, read news articles, created papier-mache, and completed crossword puzzles.

By the time I reached the seventh grade, the school district started school bus service in our rural community. However, due to Jim Crow laws of segregation, black students were not allowed to ride the bus. To avoid the possibility that the school bus driver might stop and pick us up, the bus route went counter-clockwise to our walking route.

The irony is that we knew the bus driver personally. He was the son of our Polish neighbors, a young man in his 20s. A common fence line separated our property from theirs. My mother and the bus driver's mother were well acquainted. My mother, along with my younger brother Travis and me, used to cross the fence, walking up the hill carrying fresh vegetables from our garden. We'd exchange the vegetables for eggs.

ANDREW BENFORD AND A TEACHING MOMENT

My mother had four boys and one girl. The girl was the first of twins, Madelyn and Melvin. The chores of washing dishes fell on me first. Soon, it fell on my brother Travis, and then my brother Lawrence (Ben). Now there were three of us who took turns washing dishes. Washing the dishes was the toughest of the three jobs of washing, drying, and putting the dishes away. We called this wash, dry, and put up. Sometimes we argued about who would wash, who would dry, and who would put up the dishes.

One night, as we argued about whose turn it was to wash the dishes, my grandfather overheard our argument. When he realized we were at a stalemate, he intervened to settle the dispute. After a loving lecture about how we should work together, he introduced a solution. He created a system for us to use. The person who washed the dishes the previous night would dry them the next night.

The person who dried the dishes the previous night would put the dishes away the following night. The person who put the dishes away last night washed the next day's dishes. It worked. Not only did it work then, but it worked throughout our school days. It became a system we would duplicate for decades. We applied this system to our chores and activities for years. We were always looking for ways to systematize any activities that involved manual labor.

ALLWISE MISSIONARY BAPTIST CHURCH

My family was a member of Allwise Missionary Baptist. Reverend E. L. Johnson was the pastor. As a youth at Allwise Missionary Baptist Church, I participated in skits and plays for Christmas, Easter, Mother's Day, Baptist Young Peoples Union (BYPU), Sunday School, and other occasions to use my voice in praise of God and show honor and respect to the church elders. These activities instilled in me Christian values that motivate and inspire me to this day. They also helped me understand the importance of civic engagement in my community and society as a whole. This has been and remains the foundation of my theology.

HOMECOMING

The annual Homecoming is still a major celebration at Allwise Missionary Baptist Church. It takes place on the third Sunday in October, as it has for nearly a century. I was invited to be on the program in October 2019. My youngest brother, Melvin, was the guest speaker. He gave a beautiful summation of the history of Allwise, its founders, including Mr. Punch McClellan, who donated the land to build the church, and what it meant to and still means to the community; what it meant to me (us) growing up, and what it means to us today.

HOW I LEARNED TO DRIVE AT THE AGE OF 12

We were two crooks and turns from the house. My dad got out and came around to the passenger side of the truck, where I was sitting. He told me to slide over behind the wheel and told me to "drive home." He'd left the engine running. I depressed the clutch, put it in first gear, and took off smoothly. I shifted into second, then to third, and drove us all the way home without stopping.

BEHIND EVERY GOOD FAMILY, THERE'S A GOOD MOTHER

It was a family tradition to grow watermelons, tomatoes, collard greens, red potatoes, corn, squash, okra, black eyed peas, and string beans. The cows provided fresh milk and pure butter. If we owned a can opener, it was used so seldom that I don't ever remember seeing one. Our diet consisted of fresh fruits and vegetables from the garden, as well as meat from butchering a steer once a year.

My mother worked alongside my dad in the fields until we were old enough to become field hands. Then she returned to her first love, homemaking. She maintained the books and kept records of crop production, loan payments, time sheets, and tax receipts. Maintaining accurate records was critically important for a farmer.

It has been said that behind every great man there's a great woman. My mother was that woman. Her quiet strength and spirituality sustained us in seasons and out of season, through challenges and the Jim Crow era. She knew how to treat each of us differently in order to treat us equitably. She taught us patience and perseverance by example.

My mother loved to fish, and so did I. I learned to fish by watching my dad and his friends, who also loved fishing. Fishing was a sport for them, but first and foremost, it was often dinner when little else was available to eat. They fished nearby in New Year's Creek and the Brazos River.

On "good fishing days," as determined by my research in the Farmer's Almanac, my mother would tell me to go dig up some bait, earthworms, because we were going fishing. We would walk from the house to New Year's Creek to fish for perch. As the wife of a farmer, my mother sometimes ran errands and managed some of the tasks necessary to keep the farm productive and out of debt. When those times came, I rode with her in our old, dirty-red 1941 V/8 Ford pickup truck.

The entry gate to the homestead was made of wood. It dragged on the ground when we opened and closed it. My mother hated opening it. She had asked my dad multiple times to fix it. One evening, my mother and I returned home from buying groceries to find the gate closed as usual. But on this particular day, my mother was not in the mood for dealing with the gate. Instead of stopping, she matter-of-factly drove straight into it, knocking it off its hinges, flat on the ground, then, without stopping, drove over it like nothing happened.

My dad replaced it with an iron gate that lasted for 70 years.

Despite my family's success and their best efforts to raise a family the best they knew how with what they had, as my story progresses, you'll realize my life has not been a bed of roses. Two years after I returned home from Vietnam, my mother was diagnosed with terminal cancer. She'd had some health issues in the past. However, some people felt her condition was exacerbated by my tour of duty in Vietnam.

My son Malcolm was born in 1972. His mother, Pollie (whom we called Paula) and I made a trip to Chappell Hill to visit my parents. My mother's face lit up with delight when she held her firstborn grandson for the first time. Sadly, she lost her battle with cancer in 1975.

HARD TIMES

By the late 1970s and early 1980s, we were all hard at work, married, building careers, and raising our respective families. Money was tight, to say the least. With none of us around to help run the farm, it produced very little income. With just a few heads of cattle and a fixed income, it became difficult for us to keep up with the property taxes, insurance, payments on farm equipment, and a new tractor, which ultimately led to bankruptcy.

We lost the equipment and tractor, as well as most of the cattle, but were able to hold on to the land.

My grandfather, Andrew Benford, the cornerstone of our family, died in 1958.

THE BENFORD FAMILY & FRIENDS REUNION

To this day, we continue to host our family reunions, which were first organized by my grandfather, Andrew Benford, in 1956. They were held on the Fourth of July for over five decades. In 2023, due to the increasingly extreme heat in July, my siblings and I decided to relocate the Benford Family & Friends Reunion to the Saturday after Labor Day, taking advantage of the cooler weather.

Chapter 2
Train up a Child

Train up a child in the way he should go, and when he is old, he will not depart from it.

— Proverbs 22:6

One of my earliest responsibilities that I can recall was pumping water from the well and carrying buckets of water into the house for drinking, cooking, and washing dishes. I pumped water from the well by standing on top of the stone well cover to reach the pump handle.

As I grew older, I taught my two younger brothers how to do the chores, which ranged from cleaning our room to washing dishes, gathering freshly laid eggs, chopping firewood, and later feeding the hogs and milking cows. When we got older, the responsibilities became more crucial. We grazed cattle, mended old fences, and built new ones. We watered the cattle daily and fed them hay during the winter months. We loaded selected ones on the trailer and took them to the auction. We repaired our cars, trucks, and tractors. My dad taught us to do all these things.

LEARNING AND GROWING AT PETERSVILLE ELEMENTARY SCHOOL

Every morning, Mrs. Simpson, the principal, would bring a copy of the Houston Post newspaper to school. She started me doing the daily puzzles and simple science experiments, which I quickly mastered, and then moved on to more challenging puzzles and cutouts. She taught multiple classes in the two-classroom schools. Petersville was a Rosenthal school. When it was not my time to present my classwork, she allowed me to go into the book room where all of the books were stored and read any book I chose. I read a lot of books. I'm deeply grateful to her for the foundation she laid in my early childhood and for the inspiration she provided. She also taught us drama by having us learn speeches and role-playing parts in school plays. We listened to music on

Friday evenings and everyone got a free bottle of Coca-Cola.

After graduating from Petersville Elementary School in May 1958, I enrolled in the 9th grade at C.H. Hogan, Jr. High School in Chappell Hill, Texas. That's when my parents gave me the old family car. Yep, that same beige 1949 4-door sedan that we used to go to grandma's house. By this time, the school district provided the black students with a school bus. But it didn't come to our house on Allwise Road, so the only way for me to catch the school bus into town was to drive my car to meet the bus at the end of the line, about three and a half miles from our house.

With the car came responsibilities and deferred mainte-nance. I recall several instances after school when the car didn't make it home due to mechanical issues: a flat tire, a dead battery, or one time running out of gas. When the car broke down, I walked home. My brother and I would take my dad's truck to go and fix whatever the problem was, returning home sometimes way after dark.

CLASS PRESIDENT IN JUNIOR HIGH SCHOOL

My classmates elected me class president in 9th grade and again in 10th grade. As class president for our ninth-grade class, I organized a fundraiser to raise money for our 10th-grade graduation. We needed something big to get the community excited and turnout for the fundraiser. I offered to reach out to a popular disc jockey named Hotsy Totsy in Houston, 62 miles away. The class agreed. I mailed my handwritten letter at the post office on my way home. Then, after dropping the letter in the mail, I caught the school bus to my car, where I parked every morning (because the school bus did not go all the way to Allwise Road).

We could hardly contain our excitement when he responded "Yes" to our invitation. We made posters and posted them around town. Word spread throughout the Black community in Chappell Hill, a city with a population of fewer than 1,000 total residents. Some folks were doubtful that a jock as popular as Hotsy Totsy would come to our small school. Hotsy Totsy did indeed come to town. People were elated.

The school auditorium was packed. The dance floor was also packed for the entire two hours, with dancers ranging in age from 15 to 80. What a treat this turned out to be for the townspeople who had listened to him on the radio for years.

My parents were strict disciplinarians. There were serious consequences for disobeying the rules or failing to complete chores on time. That discipline ranged from a critique of my actions and a lecture to several lashings with my dad's belt. As a teenager, I was not allowed to attend dance parties with certain friends if my parents didn't approve of them or felt I might be influenced by undesirable peer pressure. One Friday night, I was all dressed up to go out with one of my friends who was a high school dropout. I remember that evening as if it were yesterday. My dad gave me an ultimatum: Go hang out at the juke joint and party with my friend, or stay home and study.

I'm ever more grateful for my dad's teaching and discipline. It kept me on the right path. For instance, he used to tell me, "You can go hang out with *them* on Friday nights, or you can go to college. The juxtapositions emphasized that we have choices in life. There are high roads and low roads. We get to choose. Our lives are a summation of the choices we make. "Don't just follow the crowd" was his mantra.

My parents taught us to say "yes, sir" or "no, sir," and "please and thank you" to our elders. One day, after we left the store with him, where he often shopped for supplies, I asked him why he said "yes, sir" and "no, sir" to young white men who were a decade or so younger than he was.

He said, "I do it so y'all won't have to." I never heard the word "inferior" come out of my dad's mouth in any context. I didn't know certain people thought I was inferior. He protected us from such negative programming. He always told us we could be anything we wanted to be. He did his part to make that belief a reality.

I was instructed and held accountable for teaching, mentoring, and protecting my younger siblings. I was also responsible for organizing and assigning chores to each of my brothers. Approximately two years apart, chores were allocated according to age and ability. As we grew older, the responsibilities became more significant. We grazed cattle, took them to the auction, cut down trees for firewood, and hauled cotton to the cotton gin.

My dad believed that if you train the oldest child in the right way, he, in turn, will lead his brothers and sisters to excel. My dad was a master teacher. He respected his elders and taught us to do the same. Out of respect and in keeping with our teaching, we always referred to older people as Mr. and Mrs. or Miss.

A good example of the effectiveness of his teaching happened one day, while my brother Travis and I were working at the cotton gin. The weightmaster, looking at the trailer of cotton that was next in line, asked Travis, "Whose cotton is that?"

"It belongs to Mr. Columbus," Travis replied. He pondered my brother's answer for a few seconds, trying to figure out what white man Travis was referring to.

Then the light bulb went on. "You talking 'bout Columbus Colman?" (who happened to be black).

"Yes, sir," my brother replied. He walked away looking perplexed. The moral of the story is that my dad taught us to say "yes, sir" and "no, sir" to our elders, regardless of their creed or color. We gave the elders the respect they deserved. "Yes, sir," "no, sir," "Mr," and "Mrs" were not platitudes reserved for whites only. We showed respect for all elders. We still do, and we'll continue to teach it to our children.

By studying diligently and being obedient to my parents' instructions, I was advanced to the class section that my high school English teacher, Mrs. Gladys Hogan, referred to as her "college-bound students." I was fortunate to have excellent teachers from elementary through high school. Teachers like Mrs. Maggie Simpson in the 4th through 8th grades. Mrs. Gladys Hogan for English; Mr. Henry Petty, math; Mr. Lorenzo Cole, History; Coach Henry Rogers, football; Mr. Little and Mr. Thomas in the Agriculture department. They taught us lessons above and beyond the textbooks.

GRADUATING FROM HIGH SCHOOL

I graduated from Pickard High School in June 1962 in the top 20 percent of my class. In September of 1962, I enrolled in Prairie View A&M University, where I majored in Industrial Education with a minor in Business. I'm super proud and deeply grateful to have attended a historically black college. I was fortunate and thankful to be supported financially by my parents and brothers, who worked the farm, and my part-time work, first as the Layout Editor for the school newspaper, The Panther, then at the dining hall bussing tables.

The head of the publication department at Prairie View, Dr. C.A. Woods, was also the local official representative for Little League Baseball Inc., headquartered in Williamsport, Pennsylvania. Dr Woods held regular meetings with all the team managers in the area, including my dad and me, who managed one of the seven teams.

COACHING LITTLE LEAGUE BASEBALL WITH MY DAD

In his younger days, my father was an avid sandlot baseball pitcher. Friends and relatives have shared with us on numerous occasions that he was most likely destined to play in the Negro Leagues before he suffered an injury to his throwing arm. He was a right-handed pitcher and could throw a curve ball with a two-foot break.

My dad, Finis Roland Benford, never had the chance to play in the Major Leagues, but he remained an avid baseball fan for years. He was a big fan of the New York Yankees. His dislike for the Brooklyn Dodgers was well known. In 1961, he invested his love for the game into leading the effort to organize the first-ever official Little League and Pony League baseball teams in the Chappell Hill community. I coached alongside my dad from 1961 to 1964. I went off to college in 1962. By 1965, most of the Pony League players had aged out of the league and were playing high school baseball teams. There was no one else to take my place coaching with my dad. Most of the Pony League players aged out. By the end of the year in 1964, our team ended its historic run.

Our team was made up of kids who had only played softball during recess and PE at school, and kids who had never played baseball before. We trained and coached those kids not only to be competitive but to win two championships.

With my dad as manager and me as the coach, I was responsible for driving our pickup truck to pick up the players, holding practice on Tuesday and Thursday evenings after school, and driving them all back home after practice. I'd repeat the process on game day, Saturdays.

My dad recruited kids for the team, made and enforced the rules, trained the pitchers, and maintained pitcher rotation. Practice was not just about technique but included instilling discipline, mental conditioning, and resilience. We practiced hard. I stressed the basics and used situational scenarios to prepare the kids for how to respond to situations they were sure to encounter during the game.

GAME DAY

On game day, I made the lineup based on observations made during practice. I'd assign a player to keep the scorebook. I also managed the dugout and the base coaches, who were often the players themselves. Pops trained and managed the pitchers, determined pitcher rotations, gave the signs to the batters, and called out players on either team when they displayed unsportsman-like conduct.

I picked up each kid from their home, covering a seven-mile radius, and drove them home after practice and after each game because parents were working and could not afford the time off during the week. I didn't mind. It was my contribution to the team, the league, and the future success of the young players. My inspiration also came from the fact that the players were as dedicated as I was. I never had to wait for any one of them when I drove up to their house to pick them up.

They were always ready and excited to practice or play on game day. I loved working with them because these guys were committed and tough-minded. They all were coachable, disciplined, and trusted our coaching decisions. Their positive attitudes and desire to win made all the difference. That made it all worthwhile for me. This was the key to our success. We won two championships and one all-star tournament in 4 years. Not bad, considering half of the team had never played organized baseball before.

In addition to our team, the Chappell Hill Nastros, the other teams were Brenham, which had two teams, Hempstead, Belville, Bryan, and Old Washington. Both Little League and Pony League teams always played back-to-back on game day, with Little League first. There were day and night games. We traveled over a 50-mile radius to compete during playoff games.

Pops taught the pitchers how to throw his famous curve ball, both breaking in and breaking out of the strike zone. As a result of his injuries, he was very protective of the throwing arm of each of his pitchers. He knew his career-ending injuries were caused by throwing too many curve balls and not resting long enough between games.

He taught them how to throw a curve ball using the grip on the ball with the index or middle fingers on the seams. When thrown with a downward motion and enough velocity, the ball will spin, breaking in or out depending on which finger you used as the ball left your hand. This method of throwing a curve ball involves cocking and twisting the wrist and rotating the forearm to impart enough spin to cause the ball to break. This technique also concealed the pitch from the batter. One of our pitchers, Ira Newsome, employed this technique to win games in high school and college at Prairie View A&M, leading his team to the Nationals, where they were ultimately outplayed.

OUR BASEBALL CAPS WERE OUR UNIFORMS

In 1961, our first year in the newly organized league, we didn't have official uniforms. But we were not deterred. We trained and coached them, and with the full support of parents and the community, they developed a mental toughness that allowed them to tune out the noise and hone their focus on being the best they could be. Our baseball caps with the team name on them were our uniforms.

In the second year, we wore our new baseball caps with the team name on them, cutoff blue jeans, and white T-shirts. We beat the Brenham Blue Jays to win our first championship. The following year, we gained a sponsor named Mrs. Ira Mae Newsome, whose son, AJ, played second base on our team. New uniforms took the teams' efforts and commitment to a whole new level. And in the 1964 season, we won our second championship with a win over our staunch rival, coach Frank Yep's team from Hempstead. Our team also won one All-Star Tournament, beating Bellville's All-Star team. Our team produced many successful players, both on and off the field.

Roosevelt Leaks, whom I taught to play first base in Little League, was accepted to the University of Texas at Austin, where he became an All-American running back and was inducted into the College Football Hall of Fame in 2005. Roosevelt was drafted by the Baltimore Colts and played from 1975 to 1979. He played for the Buffalo Bills from 1980 to 1983.

Cecil Cooper, our opposing first baseman, was the youngest of three brothers, John Cooper and Sylvester Cooper. John was my best friend in high school. Ceicil became an All-American Professional baseball player, manager, coach, and sports agent. He played in the majors from 1971 to 1987 for the Boston Red Sox. His team won the 1975 American League Pennant. He was a 5-time American League All-Star and RBI Champion. He later became the batting coach and the manager of the Houston Astros.

Eric Himphill, my alternate first baseman's grandson, is a star football player for Brenham High. He is an All-District cornerback ranked by 247Sports as No. 39 CB and the No. 61 Overall player in the state of Texas.

Melvin Benford, our Pony League first baseman, graduated from the University of Texas-Pan American with a Master's degree in Education. He taught and coached in middle and high schools in the Rio Grande Valley. He became a successful educator and retired as a principal at one of the nation's highest-performing middle schools.

Although my dad never got to play in the Big Leagues, he instilled his talent and passion for the game in us and a group of eager youths who accepted what he had to offer and took his input to a whole new level.

Youth sports reveal and build character, good sportsmanship, and develop leadership skills, not only in the players but also in the coaches. Kids learn to accept responsibility and to be held accountable. Winning and losing teach them how to accept success and failure and appreciate the lessons learned from both. We learn more from failure than we do from winning. The players learned to listen to their coaches and trust the process. Our players' positive attitudes and desire to win made all the difference. That made it all worthwhile for me, too.

FAMILY HISTORY THAT SHAPED MY FUTURE

I was blessed to grow up with a deep and broad knowledge of my family's history, going back to slavery on my dad's side of the family, and four generations dating back to 1862 on my mother's side. Gratefully, this history was generally shared orally by my dad, grandfather, uncles, aunts, and elders in the community through stories, corroborated by eyewitnesses and others who lived in Chappell Hill and on plantations during and after slavery, as well as through the Jim Crow era.

Census records provided additional information. For the formerly enslaved people in the South, the difference between progress and poverty was ownership of land. Under the Revenue Act of 1862, the Union seized land from Southern landowners who did not pay taxes to the Union. When the Emancipation Proclamation was passed in 1863, formerly enslaved people were able to purchase land at the tax auction. Blacks began farming the land they bought. The original owners were later compensated for their land through successful lawsuits.

My dad shared with us that Uncle Joe B. Wilburn, my dad's mother's brother, was born in 1865, the year slavery ended. Therefore, Uncle Joe B's parents were enslaved. This rich history gives me a profound sense of who I am and also instills in me a sense of belonging. My ancestors were survivors. My values and ideals of community involvement were inspired by community leaders like Uncle Joe B. Wilburn and his sons Eugene and Matt Gaines Wilburn, Punch McClellen, Annie Mae (Benford) Williams, and Andrew Benford.

Matt Wilburn, my dad's first cousin, was named after the first African American state senator from Washington County, Matthew "Matt" Gaines. Matthew Gaines, a leader in the black community, was a minister and politician. He utilized his knowledge of the Land-Grant Act of 1862 to assist the Texas state legislature in establishing the Agriculture and Mechanical College of Texas, which later evolved into Texas A&M University. This effort established a path for thousands of farmers and other workers to gain access to higher education in Texas.

There were other role models as well, such as Booker Hogan, the local mortician, Eddie Harrison, county extension agent, superior court judge, and historian,

Columbus Coleman, farmer; my grandmother, Nicie Malone, a housewife, and Maggie Simpson, a teacher and principal. My first pastor was Reverend E.L. Johnson. This community of elders demonstrated family values and shaped my future. This community also taught and lived the Fruit of the Spirit. Finally, they taught me the importance of civic responsibilities, education, and instilled in me self-confidence and self-initiative. I'm grateful for my upbringing. It was the foundation for me to align my actions with my life purpose.

A BRIEF HISTORY OF SHARECROPPING

My dad got his start in farming by working as a sharecropper until he could afford his own tractor and farm equipment. Sharecropping is a financial arrangement between the landowner and the tenant in which the tenant plants cotton on a set number of acres. The typical sharecropper lives on the land he farms and shares the harvest with the owner in a 50/50 split. The difference between my dad and other sharecroppers was that he owned his land but chose to work for Robert Schaer, who owned hundreds of acres of farmland called "the bottom." We lived on our land in our house, and that provided a safe and secure environment for us to grow up in.

Sharecropping was implemented after the Emancipation Proclamation in 1863. The Proclamation was signed into law by President Abraham Lincoln on January 1, 1863, during the Civil War. After enslaved people were freed in 1865, sharecropping provided a means for them to eke out an existence in the post-slavery Antebellum South. Oftentimes, newly freed slaves worked the same plantation land on which they had previously been enslaved. When the crops were gathered and sold in the Fall, the tenant "settled up" with the landowner and usually wound up in debt and had to borrow against next year's crop to survive the coming winter months.

However, my dad, with two years of college under his belt, and my mother, who kept the books, he was able to avoid the slippery pencil that kept others in debt year after year. The sharecropper bore all expenses from cotton seeds to labor. One day, I asked my dad why he worked for Robert Schaer. He told me this was a way to have access to capital. With access to capital to fund cotton farming, he could use his resources to maintain his household and send his children to college.

My dad was one of three tractor drivers for Robert Schaer. They did the tractor work for all of the sharecroppers in "the bottom." The three of them worked the fields according to the season from sunup till sundown, five days a week. They planted, plowed, cultivated, sprayed for boll weevils, hauled cotton to the cotton gin, mowed cotton stalks after the harvest, and tilled the land for the next year's crop. By the time I was twelve, I was also driving tractors during the summer.

The relationship between Finis Benford and Robert Schaer began sometime around 1939, when my dad was standing with a group of men looking for work. Robert Schear drove up and said he was looking for workers. "I need men with strong backs and weak minds." If you want to work, step forward. My dad just stood there. He asked my dad why he didn't step forward. "Don't you want to work?" he asked.

"Yes," my dad replied. "I have a strong back, but I don't have a weak mind."

Robert Schaer asked, "Can you drive a tractor?"

"Yes," my dad replied.

"Can you work Saturday?"

"Yes," he replied again.

From this response, Mr. Schaer told my dad where to find the tractor, described the location, the work to be done, and the time he wanted my dad to begin work. When Saturday arrived, my dad got on the tractor, showed up at the allotted time, and proceeded to do the work. Unbeknownst to my dad, Mr. Schaer was watching him from behind the tree line in the distance to see if he would show up on a Saturday at the appointed time and do the work.

THREE IMPORTANT LESSONS TO TAKE AWAY FROM THIS RELATIONSHIP

Finis Benford's first economic step was to refuse to answer the call to step forward for work when the call was for "strong backs and weak minds."

A good work ethic and honesty always pay dividends. My dad was asked to work on a Saturday, and he showed up, did the work, unsupervised. Later that evening, Mr. Schaer revealed himself to my dad and told him he had been watching him. That day, he hired my dad as a supervisor.

Honesty and integrity create trust. Mr. Schaer believed he could trust my dad with the maintenance and care of his tractors, paying the workers, overseeing fuel delivery, storage, and usage.

FROM SHARECROPPER TO FARMER

Our circumstances began to change for the better when my dad and six other Black landowners organized and petitioned the Farm Service Agency for their own county extension agent. The county extension agent is a valuable resource who provides expert knowledge and current information that helps farmers increase their productivity. The FSA hired Mr. Eddie Harrison, a U.S. Army Veteran.

Working with Mr. Harrison led my dad to meet Mr. Evans, who was an administrator with the Farmers Home Administration (FHA). He controlled the grant money and payouts to farmers based on need. My dad found favor in Mr. Evans. Through his relationship with him, he gained access to the Acreage Diversion Program, which was exclusive to farmers but not available to sharecroppers. Mr. Evans helped Dad get into the program.

To maximize financial benefits, you needed to farm more land than my dad had allotted to cotton. By leasing an additional 60 acres of land to supplement the acreage he already farmed, my dad qualified for the diversion program under which Farmers were paid to let land lie out of production for a year voluntarily. This calculated move elevated my dad from sharecropper to Certified Farmer. Being certified as a farmer provided access to operating capital and loans for farm equipment.

In 1953, my dad purchased a new Ford tractor. Although he had ended his tenure as a sharecropper, he continued his relationship with Robert Schaer, who was the president of the Farmers National Bank (now known as Chappell Hill Bank). Established in the late 1800s, it was the oldest continuously operated bank in the nation during the 1950s.

Eight years later, my dad purchased a John Deere cotton picker, effectively ending the dependence on the dwindling number of manual laborers for gathering the cotton crop. This brought an end to a generation of cotton pickers, freeing us up to start school in September like the rest of the kids. The arrival of the cotton picker provided us with the opportunity to organize ourselves into a team. We implemented systems to support the driver and perform maintenance on the cotton picker.

I was the driver, and my brothers provided the ground support, which included refueling, refilling the 50-gallon water tank to keep the spindles clean, switching trailers full of cotton for empty ones, and hauling cotton to the gin. This maximized uptime and allowed the cotton picker to run from morning, after the cotton was dry, to dark. This system was an extension of the dishwashing system taught to us by our grandfather when he heard us arguing about whose turn it was to wash the dishes.

I worked summers driving tractors, chopping cotton for two dollars a day, picking cotton for two dollars per hundred pounds, and working at the cotton gin. Driving tractors and working at the cotton gin paid three dollars a day. Cotton was our cash crop, and cultivating and growing it meant missing the first three weeks of school to harvest the time-sensitive cotton crop.

As far back as I can remember, we raised cattle for food, milk, and to sell for cash. As I mentioned earlier, when Spring arrived, we would round up some cows and take them to the auction. This provided some much-needed cash after lean winter months. We would take a steer to the butcher so we'd have fresh meat to go with fresh potatoes and vegetables from the garden. This cycle repeated itself throughout my childhood and into my first years at Prairie View.

By the time I was a Junior at Prairie View, my dad had three sons in college. The farming duties and responsibilities fell entirely on my dad and baby brother, Melvin. Pops had purchased a new Ford tractor, the Model 6000. It was big; a real workhorse with a 6-speed automatic transmission. It made the work at the farm easier, but as my brother Melvin reminds us when we talk about those days, he did the work of three people: me, Travis, and Lawrence.

Cotton farming in the 1940s and 50s was an arduous occupation, yet it had its rewards. It was entrepreneurial at its core, offering a degree of freedom that provided independence unavailable to those who worked 9 to 5 for someone else. For instance, when the hot weather became nearly unbearable in June, we would work early mornings and late evenings. When it got extremely hot in mid-July, we would work half days. We always stopped work on June 18th at noon and celebrated Juneteenth, as far back as I can remember. This flexible schedule did not apply during harvest time.

PICKING COTTON WITH PAPA LES

Cotton was the economic engine and the primary source of livelihood for most residents living in Chappell Hill, with its population of approximately 500 in the 1950s, down from 1,000 in 1930. Cotton farming follows the long tradition of my African American ancestors in this country. As kids, my brothers and I worked in the fields alongside a man everybody knew as Papa Les. Working in the cotton fields was all he knew. For him, it was a way of life. We considered it an honor to work alongside him. I should say behind him. Because no matter how far ahead we were, he would always catch up and pass us, whether chopping or picking cotton.

Papa Les described himself as an "ex slave." Enslaved people worked from sunup to sundown. No one doubted him since no one knew his exact age. Some said he was about one hundred years old. Simple math tells us he was the son of enslaved people. Papa Les could pick 200 pounds of cotton a day. He toiled five days a week beneath the hot sun, sweat drops falling from his face like slow-moving raindrops. I never once heard him complain.

The tools of the trade for picking cotton are a cotton sack slung over one's shoulder, knee pads, if you could afford them, and strong, swift hands and nimble fingers. Bent over at the waist, arms and fingers extended, reaching and grabbing the cotton from the bolls. Once both hands are full, the cotton is deposited into the sack. This process is repeated until the sack is full or too heavy to pull. When we got tired of bending over at the waist, we would "walk" on our knees. This method is called "crawling."

Sometimes, the field hands would sing songs, engage in conversations, tell jokes, laugh, and chat. Other times, no one said a word. In the silence, all you could hear was the rustling of the leaves on the cotton stalks and the drag of the cotton sacks. In these solitary moments, it was easy to fall into daydreaming and, for a brief while, detach from the reality of the moment, entering a stream of consciousness that felt like shaking hands with my ancestors. This feeling embodies the spirit that keeps their memory alive. There is some solace in this remembrance.

The days were hot and long. As sunset approached and the hot, dusty ridgeline turned orange, Papa Les would stand up straight, looking toward the west at the setting sun, and yell, "Go Down Hannah!" referring to the seemingly paused sunset. Sundown was quitting time for enslaved people.

Chapter 3
Navigating the Local Socio-Political Landscape in the 1960s

For I know the plans I have for you, declares the LORD, plans to prosper you and not to harm you, plans to give you hope and a future

— Jeremiah 29:11

T he population in Chapel Hill in the early 1960s was approximately 300 residents, according to the Texas State Historical Association at the University of Texas at Austin. The citizens of the town included farmers, bankers, merchants, salespeople, a postman, mechanics, schoolteachers, preachers, housemaids, field hands, ranchers, and cowboys.

The field workers, for the most part, were Black and, in my estimation, accounted for over half of the population. On Saturdays, the downtown area would be bustling with activity fueled by Black field workers collecting their week's pay, buying groceries, work clothes, cotton sacks, knee pads, and eating some of Mr. Fat's Bar-B-Que. Some would be drinking beer and dancing in the back room at Bob's place, while others just visited with each other on the sidewalks or in cars and trucks.

Jim Crow laws of segregation were not strictly adhered to by local merchants. Chappell Hill is located 57 miles northwest of Houston, just off US Highway 290. In the 1950s, Chappell was unique in that Blacks and Whites shopped at the same stores, banked at the same bank, and purchased their medicine and ice cream cones at the same drugstore. No public place in town was off limits to the Black field workers. Bob's was one of two bars downtown. It served both Blacks and Whites.

The long bar stretched from just inside the front door to the back room where the juke box was situated. Blacks entered the bar through the back room and occupied the back half of the bar. This group was composed predominantly of field hands. Whites entered from Main Street, and they all sat at the front half of the bar. My parents didn't drink or frequent the place. However, I witnessed this scene up close and personally several times when I went there on Saturdays with my dad to pay some of the field workers. My dad and I would enter through the front door.

Before some of my readers accuse me of romanticizing my past, let me take a step back and share a broader perspective on Washington County in the 1960s. This was LBJ country. Lyndon Baines Johnson was the United States Senator for our senatorial district with the intent of becoming Vice President of the United States. Johnson owned the local radio station KTBC, where his friend Dan Rather, from Austin, was the local news anchor. This relationship provided Johnson with the power he needed to control the political narrative even in Washington County. Gus Mutscher, speaker of the Texas House of Representatives, resided in Brenham, the county seat of Washington County.

This was the cast of characters who controlled the political climate and consequently the racial environment in Washington County. The message coming out of Johnson's political circles was clear. He did not want his chance of becoming vice president of the United States ruined by racial unrest or racial incidents in his district. Lyndon Johnson usually got what he wanted. To the best of my knowledge, there were no racial incidents or political violence in Washington County during the 1960s.

When Lyndon Johnson became John F. Kennedy's Vice President, JJ "Jake" Pickle, a US Representative from Texas and a personal friend of LBJ, ran for Johnson's Senate seat as planned and won. My dad campaigned for Jake Pickle. My dad and Jake Pickle met in the living room at our house on several occasions during Pickle's campaign. During one of his visits, he gave each of us a lapel pin that was a replica of a pickle.

Secondly, we lived on our land. And third, my dad was a local farmer, a member of the Masonic Lodge, and a member of the National Association for the Advancement of Colored People (NAACP). He was a community leader.

On July 2, 1964, Lyndon Johnson, President of the United States, signed the historic Civil Rights Act of 1964 into Law.

SHERIFF T.A. BINFORD RESCUES UNCLE WILLIAM

Although Chappell Hill was relatively free of racial conflict when we were growing up in the 1950s and 60s, legend has it that there was an incident that took place in Chappell Hill in 1927 that reverberated throughout the town for decades. Somebody accused my uncle William Benford of murder. An angry mob detained him. They gathered downtown on a Friday afternoon with plans to lynch him that night.

The plan was foiled when my grandmother, Sarah Benford, went to the local telephone company in Chappell Hill and asked the switchboard operator to place two long distance phone calls: one to T. A. Binford, the Harris County Sheriff at the time, and the other to my dad, who was working in Houston, and who would usually come home on Friday evenings after work.

She told the sheriff that an angry mob was planning to lynch Uncle William (my grandfather's brother). My dad said she told him not to come to Chappell Hill that evening because "there was going to be trouble in town." The sheriff and seven deputies arrived later that evening in two police cars, according to my uncle Gussie Bouldin, a fact corroborated by other townspeople. With guns drawn, they ordered the angry mob to stand down.

They put Uncle William in one of the cars and drove him to safety. For years, no one, except close relatives, knew where they took Uncle William. I don't know if his case ever went to court. I do know he lived the rest of his life as a free man.

The building that used to house the Bell Telephone Company, where my grandmother placed those two urgent phone calls, is still standing. It, like most of the old buildings downtown, is designated a historical site.

CHAPELL HILL, WHERE MY ROOTS RUN DEEP LIKE A TREE PLANTED BY THE WATER

Chappell Hill is the last town of rolling hills and valleys nestled along U.S. Highway 290 before the flatlands that host the Brazos River. It is situated along the corridor that runs between Austin, the capital, and Houston, the largest city in Texas. My love for Chappell Hill runs deep. It is from here that I stand on the shoulders of my dad, Finis, and his dad, Andrew, who was born from the union of Robert Binford, the son of a plantation owner, and Sarah, a slave girl. Andrew grew up in Grimes County. In due season, he moved to Chappell Hill, acquired farm land outside the city limits, and built the house where my dad grew up.

Growing up in a small town where the minority held the power and segregation was the law of the land came with challenges not unlike those we sometimes encounter today, like *driving while Black*. Some people simply didn't like me because of the color of my skin. But by the grace of God, the majority of people in town chose right over wrong and good over racism and bigotry.

Most of the townspeople continue to take the high road. The younger more open-minded leaders in Chappell Hill today host a variety of cultural and tourist events that bring thousands of visitors to the town annually to attend the Bluebonnet and Scarecrow festivals, Chappell Hill Historical Society Museum, Texas Star Winery, Chappell Hill Lavender Farm, antique shops, historical sites, popular homestyle restaurants and comfort food venues like Beavers Kitchen, Grapevine on Main, and Chappell Hill Barbecue & Bakery. Chappell Hill Sausage Restaurant. Local farmers and ranchers supply fresh meat and vegetables to these places. And that good ole Texas hospitality keeps visitors and native sons like me coming back again and again.

PRAIRIE VIEW A&M UNIVERSITY

In the Fall of 1962, I enrolled in Prairie View A&M University. I returned home during the summer to help my dad with coaching the Little League and Pony League teams. By 1965, the Pony League players had aged out of the league and were playing for Brenham High School. There was no one else to help my dad coach the teams. That was the end of a good run. Coaching alongside my dad and training these young guys to be competitive in organized baseball, with its stringent rules and regulations, was a rewarding experience.

Sending me off to college was costly. The added expenses of tuition, books and supplies, clothes, and food took a financial toll on the family budget. In addition to the expenses, my dad lost his oldest and most experienced farm worker. My three brothers eventually picked up the slack. This scenario would play out again in two years, when my brother, Travis, went off to college, followed by Lawrence, leaving Melvin and my sister, Madelyn, to pick up the slack for the three of us. Melvin persevered, but he reminds us to this day how challenging it was for him to fill the void left by the three of us.

At PVAMU, I was a member of the R.O.T.C. during my first and second years and completed the required two years of military training. I studied hard and got good grades for my first and second years. In the third year, though, I began to slack off in my studies. I played a lot of bid whist and ping pong at night in the rec center. For those who are not familiar, Bid Whist is a card game that involves bidding on the number of books to be made. It is played by four people, two sets of partners.

Then the bottom fell out of my GPA. By the end of my junior year, I found myself on academic probation and was unable to enroll for the Fall 1967 semester. My parents were notified that my draft number would come up sometime within the next several months. And sure enough, it did.

LIFE AFTER PRAIRIE VIEW

During the Summer of 1967, anticipating being drafted, I went on an excursion to my grandfather Andrew's hometown of Dallas. There, I met a group of friends, and together we decided to be adventurous and drive to California. We found a "Drive A Way" (a car that needs to be delivered) and drove it to California.

We arrived in Berkeley, California, in the summer of 1967. My friends dropped me off in Emeryville, and they then continued to San Francisco, delivering the car and confirming that the flat we had been promised before we left Dallas was still available. I got directions to Ashby Avenue from a police officer and headed to my uncle Gussie's place. I hadn't seen him since he visited my dad in Chappell Hill in the mid-1950s. It was a good reunion.

He wanted to know what it was like for me growing up in Texas. We talked about the old times he spent with my dad when they were growing up in Chappell Hill. He was an excellent cook. We ate soul food and talked until it was time for bed. He was just as I had remembered him when he came to visit us in Texas. He was a large man, self-educated, with a deep, resonant voice. He worked in construction as a laborer, made good money, and had good medical and retirement benefits. He was well-dressed, wearing Brooks Brothers suits and Stacy Adams shoes on weekends. He met his wife, Aunt Emogene, whom he had known since they both worked at the Naval Supply Center in Oakland. She was a tall woman, quiet with a friendly voice and a calm smile.

Uncle Gussie Bouldin was a WWI veteran and also served with the Buffalo Soldiers. The Buffalo Soldiers Division was formed in 1866, primarily composed of African American soldiers from the 9th and 10th Cavalry Regiments of the U.S. Army. They were responsible for supporting westward expansion and "protecting settlers from the (American) Indians." That's a whole other book. He shared with me that the American Indians gave them the name "Buffalo Soldiers."

He described how, in winter, the soldiers wore large army jackets with big fur hoods and lapels, with big collars enveloping their dark faces and woolly hair. When riding toward them, the indians said they looked like buffalo. Later that week, I joined my friends at the upstairs flat on Steiner Street in San Francisco's Fillmore District.

THE SUMMER OF LOVE

The Steiner Street flat was within walking distance of the Pan Handle Park and Haight-Ashbury districts, and was one block directly behind the historic Fillmore Auditorium. I recall falling asleep at night listening to live performances of some of the top groups of that era. Although the auditorium was only a block away, I never spent much time there other than to pop in occasionally to see who was playing. One section of the dimly lit auditorium resembled a large living room, complete with oversized lounge chairs and sofas. Admission was free on weeknights.

Droves of young people and tourists from all over the country congregated in the Haight-Ashbury District. Most of my days were spent exploring San Francisco. I was fascinated (and still am) by the Pacific Ocean. I spent lots of days at Playland at Ocean Beach. Playland was an iconic amusement park just North of Golden Gate Park.

It has a fascinating history dating back to WWII, when families and sailors from all over the world came to have fun on bumper cars, the roller coaster, and the Fun House, enjoying all sorts of whimsical activities. A historical account by the San Francisco History Center of the SF Public Library sums up my sentiments better than

I can express in retrospect: "Anyone who remembers Playland is wistful, or maybe just nostalgic for the gritty, blue-collar San Francisco. It wasn't just toys for the rich. It was toys for Everyone." Playland, as the name would imply, was a place of fun and merriment.

At night, I got off the streets and hung out with my housemates at the Steiner Street house. There was never a dull moment there. Jimi Hendrix, Janis Joplin, and Jefferson Airplane were all over the airwaves and were frequently played. There was always someone dropping in to hang out, smoking a joint, and listening to music.

October ushered in Indian Summer, a time when San Francisco has its warmest weather. Indian Summer is a term that originated with native Americans. According to my research, they believed that the gods sent the warm weather to allow them time to hunt and gather what they needed to survive the long winter months. Some see the term as stereotyping, much like the term "sitting Indian style" and a few other terms. I happen to believe "cancel culture" has gone overboard.

With my savings all but depleted and the Draft looming, I took advantage of the opportunity to sell Black Panther Party newspapers. I noticed that some guys who weren't part of the Panther organization were involved. I learned that anyone could visit the printing companies where the paper was printed and purchase as many bundles as they wanted for $4 per bundle. If my memory serves me correctly, you made two dollars a bundle. Tourists bought them up as fast as we could make them available. They would often give me tips. It was a good hustle.

DRAFT NOTICE FOR THE U.S. ARMY

Once I was settled in at the Steiner Street house, I wrote to my parents and gave them my address in San Francisco. In early October, I received a letter from my mother. In it was the draft notice. The notice ordered me to report to the Oakland Army Induction Center, located at 1515 Clay Street, Oakland, California, on October 26, 1967, at 5:00 A.M.

On October 25th, with my draft notice in hand, I packed my few belongings and headed to my uncle's apartment in Berkeley. Gussie and I talked about the Vietnam War. He told me that many men in California who opposed the war were moving to Canada. He asked me if I wanted to go to Canada to avoid Vietnam. He offered to pay my way and provide me with seed money to survive until I found work. I had already made up my mind to honor the notice and respectfully declined his offer. We went to bed.

THE OAKLAND INDUCTION CENTER AND ANTI-WAR PROTESTS

Having spent nearly three months living in the Fillmore District in San Francisco and hanging out in the Haight-Ashbury District, I was unaware of the magnitude of opposition to the Vietnam War. There was no television set in the Steiner Street house. Little did I know that all hell had broken out at the Induction center six days before I arrived.

According to the November issue of The Movement Press newspaper, "from 5:00 A.M. to 10:30 A.M. on October 20, 1967, 10,000 people occupied and held 22 blocks of downtown Oakland against 2000 police. The cops were outflanked, outnumbered, and out-run. People had barricaded the streets with cars, trucks, concrete bus benches, potted trees, parking meters, street signs, trash boxes, and lumber in the path of the buses carrying draftees to the Oakland Induction Center," according to The Movement Press newspaper article dated November 1967.

I was about to enter one of the most unpopular wars in American History. By 4:00 p.m. on the evening of October 26, 1967, I had taken the United States Armed Forces Oath of Enlistment and was bound for Fort Lewis, Washington, for basic training. After my first week in basic training with Bravo Company of 192 recruits, I, along with six other recruits, was called in to personnel and offered the opportunity to enlist for a 3-year term of service in exchange for a Military Occupational Skill (MOS) of our choosing. I chose Small Missile Systems Repair. The reason we were selected to enlist after being drafted, according to my interview with personnel, was because of our high aptitude scores.

U.S. ARMY BASIC TRAINING

Army basic training lasted 10 weeks, 10 hours a day. We trained in winter weather with temperatures as low as 16 degrees Fahrenheit. Next came my Advanced Individual Training (AIT), which lasted 13 weeks at Redstone Arsenal, Alabama, after a 30-day leave to visit family. I earned a Certificate in Electronics.

Two years of ROTC at Prairie View A&M made me a standout among recruits. I quickly moved up from buck private to private first class and then to platoon leader. A Platoon in basic training consisted of four squads of 12 men each for a total of 48 men. As platoon leader, my responsibilities included rousing troops for reveille, ensuring they were present and accounted for in all assemblies, and reporting this to the company commander. I lead drills designed to simulate combat situations and to prepare the barracks for inspection. I was held accountable for their performance in and out of formation.

After completing basic training, I was given leave with orders to report to Redstone Arsenal, Alabama, within 30 days for Advanced Individual Training (AIT). The 35-40 degree weather was a welcome change. The training was rigorous, consisting of eight hours a day for 13 weeks, during which I troubleshooted and repaired electronic guidance control mechanisms for anti-tank missiles. I finished the course and was awarded a certificate in electronics.

After AIT, I received a 30-day leave with orders to report to Fort Sill, Oklahoma, within 30 days. Fort Sill is one of the most important military bases in the United States. It is the home of the United States' 31st Air Defense Artillery School and the 75th Field Artillery Brigade. For me, the company of men I was stationed with was a training ground for combat service in Vietnam. It was here, at the urging of a young Lieutenant who asked me to work for him in personnel, that my military occupational skill (MOS) changed, and I was assigned to work in personnel when I arrived in Vietnam.

MY VIETNAM EXPERIENCE - LIFE IN THE COMBAT ZONE

In November 1968, after a month-long leave spent with my family in Chappell Hill, I boarded a plane in Houston for a flight to Fort Lewis, Washington. There, I joined 204 other soldiers who boarded a World Airways stretched DC-8 passenger jet bound for Cam Ranh Bay in the Republic of South Vietnam.

On landing, I realized my life had taken a turn that would usher in an unimaginable journey of uncertainty and life and death challenges. But I was not afraid. It would be a year before I saw my parents again.

On our final approach to landing in Cam Ranh Bay, the Captain turned off the lights inside the cabin as well as all exterior lights and landed on a dimly lit runway. Once on the ground, we were herded into barracks, amidst the thunderous sound of bombs being dropped by B-52s. We were issued camouflage fatigues and sent to barracks assigned for new arrivals.

The next morning, a group of other young men and I were airlifted to the Americal Division Headquarters in Chu Lai. I was assigned to the Headquarters & Head-quarters Company, 11th Infantry Brigade, at Duc Pho, a Landing Zone (LZ) located about a quarter mile from a small village 40 miles North of Chu Lai. Here I was issued an M-16 rifle, ammo, hand grenades, a flak jacket, a gas mask, and a vial of water purification tablets. I was assigned the duties of company clerk.

Eight months later, I was promoted to personnel specialist with a secret security clearance and reported directly to Captain Joe Cleary, the company commander. I made many trips between Duc Pho and Chu Lai to division headquarters, carrying time-sensitive documents, personnel orders, and messages too sensitive to transmit over unsecured temporary telephone lines and regular mail. They had to be hand-carried.

Sometimes the round trip would take several days, hitching rides on supply helicopters and Chinook troop carriers that sometimes detoured to pick up troops in hostile landing zones (LZs) because they were low on supplies or needed to be airlifted immediately due to injuries or other health-related issues. Sometimes I lucked out and traveled aboard a fixed-wing C-130 or C-140. They flew directly to the base camp, which was much faster and safer.

The American Division, in which I served, was commanded by General Westmoreland and later General Colin Powell. Those of us who worked in the base camp during the day were responsible for perimeter guard duty

3 to 4 nights a week. It was my duty as a SP-5 to assign perimeter guard duty for the 10 bunkers along the East perimeter, with three men assigned to each bunker. One stayed on guard while two slept, then rotated one at a time for two-hour shifts. This allowed the troops who fought in the field during the day to sleep in the camp safely through the night. Some troops spent several days in foxholes and trenches before coming into the base camp to rest.

While on guard duty during the dark of the moon, I could barely see my hand at arm's length in front of my face. On nights like this, we would call the operations center and request a "free fire." Once it was determined that no allied or US troops were in the area bunkers on a given perimeter (10 bunkers approximately 50 yards apart), we were allowed to fire our M16s at will into the dark abyss for two to three minutes before the other two soldiers lay down to sleep.

We Americans paid a heavy price for our participation in the Vietnam War. Over 2.5 million American soldiers served in Vietnam. Fifty-six thousand were killed. Over 150,000 wounded, 1,600 missing in action.

In a twist of Irony, after returning from the war and settling in Oakland, my next-door neighbor for ten years was a Vietnamese family. We spoke often. They were warm and friendly. I never told them I was a Vietnam veteran. As of this writing, there is a daily flight from Oakland, California, to Ho Chi Minh City, Vietnam! Several of my real estate clients are Vietnamese. What is now Ho Chi Minh City was formerly known as Saigon until the fall of South Vietnam in 1975.

During the last six months of my 18-month tour, I was allowed to choose my duties. I decided to run the Enlisted Men's Club, where we sold beer and soda to weary troops who had spent most of the day in battle in the "boonies," aka the jungle. As a way to entertain the troops, I contacted radio station KILT in Houston, Texas, and requested a Texas State Flag, which they gladly mailed to me along with a reel of Top 40 music. I played music at night from the reel while troops shared stories of battles they'd fought that day. It was here that I learned of the death of two comrades, Johnnie Johnson and Robert Montgomery. Johnnie Johnson, a door gunner on a Huey helicopter, was killed when it was shot down by enemy fire. His was the last chopper in a daisy chain formation on their way back to the base.

A few days later, we got the news that Robert Montgomery was killed by a sniper while walking as a rear point guard with his squad. The EM club offered a relative degree of safety, comfort, and camaraderie for soldiers who had survived another day of fighting in the jungle while answering the call of duty some 10,000 miles from home.

Beer and soda were in high demand. Delivery to outlying base camps was the responsibility of the Army Transportation Division. These brave soldiers transported beer and soda by tractor-trailer rigs over 40 miles of treacherous, partially paved, and dirt roads between Chu Lai and our LZ in Duc Pho. Roads were sometimes booby-trapped with land mines, and sometimes the convoy was ambushed.

Inspired by the challenges, we never went more than a day without beer and soda. Part of my daily duties was to take the company jeep, pick up the mail, then go into the nearby village, which was less than half a mile away, and buy ice to chill the beer and soda made available to soldiers during the evening in the EM Club. The daily trip to the village was a high-risk assignment. Both friendly ARVN and Viet Cong soldiers lived in the town. The merchants knew me, and by the grace of God, kept me safe from harm and possibly death.

The eighteen months I served in Vietnam were a series of life-changing experiences and a plethora of emotions. Post-Traumatic Stress Syndrome is just one of the many invisible injuries so many of us came home with. But I won't complain. In the words of the British author,

Charles Dickens, "it was [in a strange way] the best of times and the worst of times." Each day in a war zone is lived with incredible intensity and appreciation for being alive.

I learned to find joy in the simplest things that we often take for granted when we're in the safety and comfort of our homes. In a combat zone, lifespans are measured in months, weeks, and days depending on one's MOS (Military Occupational Skill). Under these circumstances it was easy to find joy in a cold soda, a letter from home, a smile, a care package of one's favorite food, a brother's dap (fist pounding) as he steps off a helicopter after surviving a battle where neither of us knew when they left that morning if they would come back alive or dead often brought unspeakable joy to me and others working in the base camp.

One of my duties as a personnel specialist with Headquarters & Headquarters Company, 11th Infantry Brigade, was to account for every soldier under our command on the Morning Report, to prepare orders for the company commander's signature for leave time, reassignments, orders to return home to the states, and to track each soldier's status daily. This included those Present and Accounted for, Missing In Action (MIA), Wounded In Action WIA), Killed In Action (KIA),

Absent Without Leave (AWOL), On Leave, or in the stockade.

I, along with my counterpart, Bill Grimes, was also responsible for any correspondence between HQ & HQ Company, as well as other units under our command. Bill Grimes and I were each awarded the Vietnam Service Medal, the Army Commendation Medal, and the Bronze Star Medal for Meritorious Service, as was Gary Palmer, who preceded Bill and me in the same capacity. Gary trained Bill and me to do the job the same exemplary way he'd performed it, by the book.

The courage and camaraderie I experienced among soldiers of all ethnicities, races, and backgrounds was a level of bonding that could last a lifetime. Here, men were ready to die, willing to die, and often did die to save the lives of others. For instance, Medevac helicopter pilots, also known as "Dust Off Crews," were responsible for flying into active combat zones and extracting wounded soldiers under fire. Medevac helicopters were unarmed and lacked door gunners; they displayed only the Red Cross insignia on the nose and sides of the aircraft.

In contrast, I witnessed soldiers' fear, insubordination, strife, and court martials; men who refused to fight any more, or chose to get high on Quaaludes, a sedative-hypnotic drug that produces a feeling of euphoria, slows the pulse rate, lowers anxiety and leads to a state of drowsiness; and men who chose to go AWOL rather than partake in the war. On the Morning Report, I accounted for soldiers who went AWOL, were captured, killed in action, or were missing in action. Some men who went AWOL were rumored to have left the war zone for Saigon, never to be seen again. These were the worst of times.

The First Sergeant generally reviewed the Morning Report and then submitted it to the Company Commander, Captain Joe Cleary, every morning. Sometimes the Captain requested the report directly from me. In cases of MIAs, KIAs, or injuries, the next of kin were notified through the chain of command within twenty-four hours.

Witnessing war firsthand and surviving it to tell my story is an incredible feat. I saw the courage, bravery, resilience, and triumph of the human spirit despite tragic circumstances. These experiences strengthened my faith, renewed my love for humanity, and nurtured my hope for peace. Life is sacred everywhere, regardless of physicality, race, gender, political ideology, religion, ethnicity, social class, color, or national origin. People everywhere love life and want to be free of war, tyranny, and oppression, free to worship the God of their choice. They want to work and play, love and raise families, watch them grow up, and contribute to their legacy and the better-ment of society. Everyone wants to be valued, appreci-ated, and loved. The Vietnamese people embodied this fact of life.

THE DAY EVERY VIETNAM SOLDIER DREAMED ABOUT

This is an excerpt of one soldier's description of leaving Vietnam for the United States after his one-year tour of duty was completed. He speaks for every soldier who was fortunate enough to board the "Freedom Bird."

"Every passenger had dreamt about this exact moment during the past year. It was a personal goal to walk up those stairs and board the 'Freedom Bird." Just like the final thirty minutes of our arrival flight one year ago, we were all anxious and paranoid. Some are calling out that the longer the plane stands out here in the open, the more susceptible we are to mayhem. These veterans maintained a vigil, looking through the cabin windows and glancing all about, watching for the tell-tale exhausts of tracers, rockets, and RPGs heading their way.

Everyone is squirming in their seats because they're eager to leave. Finally, the jet engines came to life, and the plane began taxiing toward the runway. Lookouts remained vigilant. Within minutes, the aircraft is airborne, lifting upward at a rapid rate of speed. Everyone is holding their breath until we are out of range of enemy fire. Not one person said a word. Then, just as the plane levels out and is cruising over the South China Sea, the cabin erupts in a tremendous cheer. We are hugging each other, smiling like Cheshire cats, and congratulating one another for surviving the nightmare. Others sat alone and cried."

— March 8, 2012 pdoggbiker
(https://cherrieswriter.com/)

The flight home for me was surreal. I felt like I was waking up from a dream. I reflected on my time there. I remembered Johnnie Johnson and Robert Montgomery, my two friends who answered the call of duty for our country, and gave their last full measure of devotion to a war they did not start, and a war we did not finish.

I arrived back in the States on June 4, 1970. We landed at Ft Lewis, Washington. Because I served an additional 6 months in Vietnam. The Army made good on its promise, and I was honorably discharged with the rank of E-5 the day I set foot on American soil. My file was closed. I was done — no reserve duty, no meetings. I was a free man.

I called my parents and told them I was back in the United States. To say they were relieved would be an understatement. My brother, Travis, drove from Texas to Berkeley, California, and met me at Uncle Gussie's. We then went back to Chappell Hill. Still jet-lagged from the nearly 18-hour flight, I was battling fatigue. I was blessed and grateful to be home, starving for companionship and a good home-cooked meal. By the grace of God, I had come full circle. Great is His faithfulness.

Chapter 4
Embracing The Success Principles Methodology

We get what we believe rather than what we want; you choose what to believe.

— Roy Benford

After completing a transformational speaker training course in January 2022 in Atlanta, Georgia, taught by Patrice Washington, I focused my search for a trainer and coach who could provide me with the tools and insights I needed to advance my coaching business. I envisioned my ideal trainer as someone who takes a holistic approach, inspiring me to grow into a more knowledgeable, power-ful, and confident trainer.

What I envisioned brought me in contact with Jack Canfield through a social media post where he talked about his new Train The Trainer Program (August 2023). That led me to become a Canfield Certified Trainer and Coach. This has taken me on a remarkable journey of self-awareness and learning that has elevated my coaching method, elevated my training skills, and taken my business to a whole new level.

The Train The Trainer program was taught by none other than Jack Canfield himself. The program is designed to train coaches to teach the *Success Principles* concepts through experiential demonstrations and client participation, enabling participants to consciously create a life of success far greater than they ever thought possible. This was the kind of transformational training I was looking for. This is my methodology.

Typical training focuses on increasing a person's knowledge, skills, and techniques. The goal of typical training is to equip a person with the necessary tools to carry out the duties and responsibilities of their job more proficiently. This training is typically accomplished through a combination of classroom learning, on-the-job training, and role-playing.

On the other hand, transformational training and coaching focus on a deeper fundamental change in participants' habits, thoughts, behavior, and mindset. It's a holistic approach where the goal is to create lasting change through methods that include spaced repetition, where instruction is spread out over time based on the theory that long-term memory benefits from instruction and events that are spaced over time. Training is engaging and learner-centric. This is the training I received during my certification to teach the *Success Principles* to others.

Implementing what I learned in the Canfield Certification Training has had a profoundly positive effect on my personal and professional life. The increased self-awareness I've achieved by applying Success Principle 1, "Take 100% Responsibility for Your Life," has been incredible. This principle serves as the foundation for implementing all the other success principles in your personal and professional life, ultimately creating the success you desire. The concept is this: You can't control the events that will inevitably occur in your life. What you can control is your response to those events. And it is your response to those events that determines the outcome. Let's unpack this concept.

When bad things happen to us, we tend to complain and blame other people, the economy, the government, or even politics for what happened to us and how *it* made us feel. These feelings are real and evoke a certain response in us only if we allow them. When we blame others for how we think or our circumstances, we're looking for solutions to our problems and what we're going through *outside* of ourselves. Blaming others for what happens to us and how we feel as a result is a distraction that robs us of the power we need to solve the problem at hand.

Taking 100% responsibility for what happens to us and how we feel as a result of an event requires us to look *within* ourselves and realize that we're creating what we experience through our thoughts and beliefs. Our thoughts control our actions. When we accept the fact that we control what happens to us by how we respond to events in our lives, we are empowered to shape our experiences, achieve success, and enhance our quality of life. In our half-day workshop, we delve deeply into this concept and other success principles, using live demonstrations and interactive audience participation to enhance the training.

For me, one of the most essential personal applications of *The Success Principles* has been retraining my inner critic — that little voice in my head — to deliver a positive message rather than a negative one. Using non-judgmental language when talking to myself has significantly reduced self-criticism and self-judgment that can lead to self-doubt and low self-esteem. Beginning with positive self-talk, I made the transition by shifting my mindset to focus on past positive experiences and solutions rather than the problem at hand. I've gained valuable insight into ways to master my own beliefs and behavior. When you apply this *Success Principle,* you take control of your life, which increases your self-awareness and helps you achieve greater success.

Success Principle 1: Take 100% Responsibility For Your Life" means you are responsible for everything you experience in life. I'm not surprised when my clients respond to this principle with "Are you kidding me?" "How can that be when there are events that happen in my life that are outside of my control?" Conventional thinking is that we do not have control over our lives because other people have choices and can make decisions that affect *us.* This is very true.

But it's also true that you have choices. Our thoughts and belief system create our experiences, as do the visual images we choose to focus on. Our thoughts, the visual images we choose to focus on, the resulting emotions we feel, and the actions we take are all within our control. While we cannot control the decisions others make or the events that occur as a result of other people's decisions, we *can* control our *response* to all of these events. When we control our response to the events, we control the outcome, and consequently, our lives.

Here is a hypothetical example of Success Principle #1, "Take 100% Responsibility for Your Life." I'm seated in a contentious board of directors meeting, and I raise my hand to be recognized to speak. But before the chairperson can acknowledge me, a young man whom I've never met and who is in the meeting for the first time says, "Don't listen to *him*. He's probably going to say something stupid like *they* always do." Ouch!

Now, how many of you reading this scenario think this statement would lower my self-esteem? I'm fairly certain most of you would agree. Here is what I want you to know about the situation I'm in: I have choices of how to respond. It doesn't matter what the young man says to me; what matters is what I say to *myself* after he stops talking, which *does* affect my self-esteem. My response determines the outcome; if I allow my inner critic to say, "OMG, how did he know that about me?" This *would* hurt my self-esteem.

But if I go inside myself and listen to my *inner coach*, who says, This man does not know you. Ignore his comments." Then his comments are just words, and his words have no power over me. My self-esteem is still intact because of how I chose to respond to the event. You see, it's not what the young man said that affects how I feel. It's what I believe to be true about myself that affects how I think about myself. All of our life experiences are the result of how we've responded to events and circumstances that we've encountered in our lives.

Massive changes are occurring in our nation and, indeed, the world at a galloping speed. There are hints of a recession, economic uncertainty, political turmoil, global warming, artificial intelligence, massive job firings, health care challenges, defunding of educational institutions, and blatant violation of constitutional rights. We're all impacted by one or more of these changes, which can be overwhelming and devastating.

Given these circumstances, the question any rational individual is asking is, how do I navigate through the chaos and survive, let alone thrive, in times like these? How am I going to carry out my agenda, send my kid to college, maintain health insurance, enjoy free speech and other constitutional rights when 'the system' is so screwed up? The deck is stacked against me.

It's easy to blame the government, your employer, the political parties, the courts, or Congress. *Those politicians are making their own rules and changing the laws that are preventing me from enjoying life, liberty, and the pursuit of happiness. They're stopping me from succeeding.*

First of all, remember that you're not alone. We're all in the same boat. And despite the chaos and disruptions, despite the stacked deck against us, some people continue to go about their business, raise their families, start new businesses, enjoy extraordinary careers, and live the life they love. These are the leaders, athletes, executives, entrepreneurs, and everyday individuals who have taken 100% responsibility for their lives. They have stopped blaming and complaining, and expelled the disempowered victim's conscientiousness that robs people of their power to succeed.

COACHING FOR SUCCESS

We are not victims of external circumstances. Since our thoughts control our actions, we can control what we choose to think and believe; therefore, we have the power to create our reality. We can use our thoughts to create new behaviors, beliefs, habits, and mindsets. In doing so, we become the architects of our future. We can decide what we want and create greater success in our personal and professional lives, disregarding the chaos and circumstances around us. I believe we're greater than our circumstances.

All successful people have at least two things in common: They have a coach, and they base their actions on a set of success principles. This is how famous leaders survive and thrive amid chaos and uncertainty.

Mastering the Core Principles of Success is the premier workshop offered by Aim High Coaching. It is designed to train others how to use their power to create greater awareness and success by applying a set of success principles to build businesses, increase income, overcome adversity, gain more self-confidence and control, and unlock their next levels of success.

WHAT MAKES A GOOD COACH GREAT

What sets my coaching apart and makes me a great coach is that I believe wholeheartedly in my clients' ability to maximize their potential. I love what I do and appreciate the trust my clients place in me and my abilities to produce transformational growth in their personal and professional lives. I love helping my clients discover their core genius by eliminating menial tasks and coaching them to focus on the 20 percent of activities that will produce 80 percent of the results. This is called the *new* 80/20 rule.

My professional processing skills enable me to respond to clients' sharing through my awareness of feelings, remaining non-judgmental, and using non-judgmental language, which creates an emotionally safe place for clients to discuss areas where they want help freely. I permit my clients to claim their worthiness, thereby bolstering their self-esteem.

I approach each session, whether it's one-on-one or group coaching, with authenticity, humor, and enthusiasm. Clients who complete my *Mastering The Core Principles of Success* workshops learn to interrupt the pattern of negative thoughts and replace them with positive thoughts and beliefs, new behaviors, and a self-image that aligns with who they want to become. This process shifts their mindset from 'want' and 'need' to opportunities and abundance.

ABOUT AIM HIGH COACHING

Aim High Coaching is a coaching and training company. Our mission is to partner with clients in a thought-provoking and creative process that empowers them to discover their inner strengths, enabling them to create the success, freedom, and quality of life they desire by applying *The Success Principles* in nine key areas of their lives. We dive deeply into each of these key areas in our workshops.

As a Canfield Certified Trainer and Coach, I utilize the proven, time-tested systems of *The Success Principles* which produce transformational growth and development in the lives of those I have the privilege of training and coaching.

Aim High Coaching offers this training in half-day workshops, multiple-day workshops, group coaching, one-on-one coaching, and transformational speaking engagements. This program is offered online and in person. Our clients include athletes, entrepreneurs, executives, real estate agents, and everyday individuals who seek to enhance their self-awareness and achieve peak performance in all aspects of their lives.

I know that when all of the success principles and concepts have been absorbed, the exercises have been practiced, and the affirmations have been memorized, there remains the most important takeaway of all: You must *take action.* You must be committed to implementing what you've learned during training.

The workbook I provide is content-rich and organized. Participation in my workshops is an exhilarating experience. I advise my clients, who in the past have waited to get their ducks in a row before implementing a prospecting system, to lean into it now. Don't wait for perfection, reassurance, or permission. Instead, *take action.* As I stated earlier: "Whatever you can do or dream you can, begin it. Boldness has genius, power, and magic in it. Begin it now."– Johann Wolfgang von Goethe

IMPLEMENTING WHAT I'VE LEARNED FOR THE BENEFIT OF MY COACHING CLIENTS

I know my business will grow only to the extent that I evolve. Ongoing transformative training and coaching are essential for all professionals if we intend to be the best of the best.

When I founded Aim High Coaching in 2022, I coined the slogan *"Redefining Coaching for a New Generation."*™ I chose that slogan because my training and coaching method is based on the Canfield Methodology. This proven coaching system has taught tens of thousands this formula for success and trained over 4,100 trainers, including me.

My examples and primary discussion center around real estate because this is where I spent the last 30-plus years of my professional career.

The Success Principles I teach participants apply to any profession. I present workshops, one-hour keynotes, half-day workshops, and multi-day training sessions for a variety of occupations seeking to achieve greater success in all areas of their lives.

I immersed myself in this program, and I'm so glad I did. It has provided me with the methods and tools necessary for the transformational approach to training that I offer. Applying the principles of this program has created lasting change in the lives of those I've trained.

After completing the Train The Trainer course and completing all of the written assignments, I officially became a Canfield Certified Trainer and Coach. The principles and methodologies of Train The Trainer provided me with the knowledge, self-improvement tools, and skills to transform my clients' belief systems in ways that will unleash their inner power and move them from where they are to where they want to be.

I've been intentional about creating a safe space in my workshops and one-on-one coaching sessions, where attendees can be authentic and share their experiences, strengths, and weaknesses without judgment or criticism. This principle has been paramount in discovering what my clients want to achieve through coaching. It helps me create a stronger coaching relationship and build trust in my coaching processes.

During certification, two powerful new tools quickly became my favorites: Laser Coaching and Coaching for Action. **Laser Coaching** helps my clients clearly define the outcome they want, identify mental, physical, or motivational blocks that may be holding them back, and identify the consequences of not taking action.

Coaching for Action is the fastest way to achieve the desired result the client is seeking. I use this coaching tool to inspire clients to think for themselves and focus on the solution rather than the challenge or problem they are facing. These two coaching tools enable me to quickly and succinctly identify the client's needs and wants, explain why these needs and wants are essential to them, and obtain a commitment from them to take the necessary action to achieve their desired outcome. This process now serves as the entry point — the first step — to enrolling in my coaching program.

I also teach the client how to use the power of feedback and accept that feedback is a valuable resource. It keeps my coaching clients on course toward achieving their goals. I use feedback to continue improving my program. I engage my audience by storytelling, humor, and modeling authenticity. I've also internalized the principle of facing my fear of failure and dispelled a host of limiting beliefs.

I've experienced my fears and taken action anyway, and this has led to me achieving my breakthrough goals. My experience has prepared me to coach my clients on how to master their fears. Be mindful that FEAR is nothing more than as the acronym points out: False Evidence Appearing Real. Faith conquers fear.

THE SUCCESS PRINCIPLES APPLIED TO MY PERSONAL LIFE

I am so grateful for all I have accomplished in the past three years of my training and coaching career. The increased self-awareness I've achieved by applying Success Principle #1 to my life has helped me take 100% responsibility for my life, where I used to think my 50% was my fair share.

This principle has taken my coaching program and me to a whole new level. I've gained greater focus and clarity on my life's purpose, and as a result, I've become a better coach. I'm now using the Canfield Success Principles in my half-day workshop titled *Mastering the Core Principles of Success.* Now I'm prepared to train others in this process.

THE INTAKE SESSION FOR NEW COACHING CLIENTS

When first I meet a coaching prospect and they express an interest in being coached I offer my services as a dynamic and dedicated partner, an active listener, who will ask them thought-provoking questions, and create a safe and non-judgemental space where I can gain clarity, identify strengths and develop strategies to overcome obstacles, and make a plan and set goals to maximize their potential. Together, we go through the following steps:

WELCOME CLIENT AND DETERMINE THE CLIENT'S DESIRED OUTCOMES FROM COACHING

After collecting some personal details and contact information, I ask the following questions to understand the client's needs and wants clearly and provide constructive feedback. Why are you reaching out for coaching? What goals do you want to achieve, long-term and short-term, and by when? What do you want to achieve from coaching? How will you measure your success/achievement of your goals?

WHAT TO EXPECT DURING COACHING

Coaching is **not** the same as advice, counseling, supervision, or therapy. A coach does not hold a position of authority over the client.

The International Coaching Federation (ICF) defines coaching as "partnering with a client in a thought-provoking and creative process that inspires the client to maximize their personal and professional potential." This is what I do. Coaching sessions are 100% confidential and non-judgmental, conducted in an emotionally (and physically) safe space where you can be open and forthcoming about what may be holding you back from unlocking your full potential. As the client, you're the expert in your life. I create a safe place for you to share your aspirations, fears, and challenges. To develop an effective coaching relationship, you must be open, introspective, and willing to explore areas in your professional or personal life that may be inhibiting your progress toward your big Why.

BEGIN ADMINISTRATIVE PROCESS; EXPLAIN COACHING AGREEMENT, PAYMENT, AND ALL LOGISTICAL CONTACT INFORMATION NEEDED BY COACH AND CLIENT

Answer any questions the client may have regarding how to book a coaching session. Confirm how we will handle missed and late sessions. Explain the coaching agreement, payment options, and billing process, and obtain the signed coaching agreement. Lastly, collect payment for the coaching session(s), program, series, or customized plan.

MY COACHING PHILOSOPHY

Honesty, integrity, and service are the cornerstones of my business. I put the client's needs ahead of my own. Win-win is the aim in all negotiations. Your success is my mission.

MY ROLE AS YOUR COACH

- I explain the session's structure and how sessions are conducted.
- I make sure you understand that your goals and focus sometimes change over time.
- Just know that ups and downs and challenges will occur, and you will be coached through any difficult circumstances you encounter.
- I will let you decide what you want to discuss, how, and when you would like to end the coaching agreement.
- I will give out assignments and provide Q&A opportunities between coaching sessions.
- I will help you set goals, stay focused, and hold

you accountable for doing what we agree you will do.

As your coach, I will help you establish strategies, find solutions, and challenge you in areas where you may be holding yourself back.

THE ROLE OF THE CLIENT

- To be open and forthcoming about your needs, strengths, challenges, and areas of improvement.
- Have the will to learn and be able to adopt a positive attitude
- Have a positive outlook on your personal life.
- Take full responsibility for decisions made, actions taken, and results obtained.
- Understand that success is directly related to the commitment you make and the actions you take.
- Help your coach understand your learning style (visual, auditory, reading, writing, and kinesthetic) and ways I can best coach you.
- Leave each coaching session with **at least** one action plan and a commitment.
- Share your biggest wins and takeaways from each coaching session.

- Gather all of the logistical and contact information we'll both need in the future and confirm the next coaching session.

Chapter 5
Shifting Careers From IT to Real Estate in a Shifting Economy

You can have everything in life you want if you will just help enough other people get what they want.

— Zig Ziglar

I started my real estate career in Marin County, California, in 1990 during a recession. The recession was caused by a combination of factors: the collapse of the savings and loan institutions and the Gulf War, which triggered inflation and rising interest rates.

The real estate market was challenging, to say the least, but I survived. This was a major victory for me, considering that seventy-five percent of new agents drop out of the business during their first year. Starting my real estate career in a down market and amid shaky consumer confidence prepared me for what was to come years later.

Shifts in the economy will occur. It's just a matter of when. The Loma Prieta earthquake in 1989 caused a temporary disruption in the market and made buyers hesitant to enter. The available supply of homes on the market declined, but the overall impact was short-term. Property values decreased, but not significantly.

Recessions, recoveries, booms, bubbles, and adjustments all present major challenges for real estate agents. Challenging times like these require agents to pivot and shift their mindset and work habits.

HOW IT ALL STARTED

After completing my pre-licensing courses at College of Marin and obtaining my salesperson's license, I joined TRI Realtors in Novato, California, where I had completed my real estate practice coursework under the supervision of broker associate Ollie Fleet.

Ollie was a listing agent. He offered me the opportunity to work as his assistant in exchange for training me in the basics of the real estate business. I maintained his files, made and confirmed appointments, and went on listing appointments with him. He worked hard every day and seemed oblivious to the declining market. I learned valuable lessons from the way he approached the business, his calm demeanor, and his optimistic attitude.

He gave me a great letter of reference stating I was a "quick study" and marveled at how well I had grasped the concepts of the challenging business of real estate. The mentoring and training I received while working with Ollie Fleet were the catalyst that jump-started my real estate career.

Working At Coldwell Banker — San Rafael, CA

After gaining some experience at TRI Realtors, I met with John Anderson, the broker at Coldwell Banker in San Rafael. The meeting went well. John acknowledged and appreciated my experience with TRI. He had high regard for my work as a computer programmer and systems analyst. However, he took issue with my short history in sales. He said, ironically, when I look back on it now, "Agents with technical backgrounds don't do well in this business. But I'm willing to take a chance on you."

I got off to a good start at Coldwell Banker. I teamed up with a mortgage loan agent from City Bank in San Rafael. Together, we published a bi-weekly newsletter,

Roy Benford's Real Estate Insight, with graphics and all original real estate-related content. We targeted military veterans and first-time homebuyers. The newsletter was a success. I closed three deals in one month.

My success caught the attention of Nancy Isles, a real estate reporter for the Marin Independent Journal newspaper. She published an article about my work with first-time homebuyers on the front page of the real estate section. This brought me more business. Over the next three years, I appeared in the paper several more times as an expert on first-time buyers.

This activity attracted the attention of Mary Kay Yamamoto, owner and broker of a small boutique office, RE/MAX of Central Marin, a little real estate power-house located in the center of Marin County. After five years with Coldwell Banker, I joined her RE/MAX office.

Working With RE/MAX East Bay Hills & Brokers & Owners Network

To everything, there is a season. Marin is a small county. It had a population of a little over 260,000 residents during this time. According to the Multiple Listing Service data, generally, 400–500 properties are sold per month. There were over 1,000 Realtors in Marin County in 1999. I reached a point where my monthly sales numbers were not growing. In 2000, I moved to Oakland, where I joined RE/MAX East Bay Hills in the Montclair District. Fae Bidgoli was the Broker/Owner. My business grew considerably. Twice, I was awarded Listing Agent of the Month during my second year in that office.

Fae recognized my leadership skills and selected me as Manager of New Agent Recruiting and Training for the office of about 20 agents. In this position, I called on prospective agents to join the Montclair office, recruited and trained new agents, and held weekly one-on-one meetings with new agents to set goals, problem-solve, and establish goals for the next week. I helped new agents organize their day, prospect for leads, and provided them with motivational support.

In addition to working with new agents, I participated in RE/MAX Brokers & Owners Network weekly conference calls to stay current with issues affecting other broker-owners in our region. What I learned on those calls, I reported to my broker, Fae, who was often too busy to attend the meetings.

Fae and I had a good working relationship. She hired me to list her $815,000 rental property in Kensington, a small upscale enclave that borders North Berkeley. By choosing me to list her property, she demonstrated her confidence in me and my abilities as an agent. For this, I remain grateful.

Fae was kindhearted, soft-spoken, and a progressive-minded businesswoman. She treated her agents like family. Here's one example: One day, the repo man came to the office to pick up my new Mercury Mountaineer because I had missed one payment, and another payment was coming due the next day. I had counted on a real estate transaction that was in escrow but hadn't closed. Essentially, I owed two payments totaling $1,030. The repo man was not taking any partial payments. It was either pay up or he was taking my SUV.

Fae overheard our conversation from her office. Unbeknownst to me, while I was arguing with the repo man, she walked across the street to her bank. When she came back, she handed me an envelope containing $1,500 in cash.

That's the kind of person she was. Being an Iranian woman in business with meager means, she could relate to missing a payment. She told me her story of coming to this country from Iran with very limited resources. She got her real estate license and started her new career. She once told me that when she first started selling real estate, she used to arrive at her listing appointments a half hour early, park as far away as time would permit, and walk to the client's house so they wouldn't see her bad-looking car.

By the time I joined her office in about 2001–2002, she was a broker driving a 750L BMW, owned two RE/MAX offices—one in Montclair and the second brokerage on Solano Avenue in North Berkeley. She sold both office locations and retired just before the real estate crash in 2008. She's the author of four books. She was a great inspiration for me and all of the agents who worked for her. Gratefully, I set my sails for a larger pond.

RE/MAX In Motion, Castro Valley, California.

By the early 2000s, RE/MAX had become known as the leader in real estate sales and technology. RE/MAX In Motion consisted of a staff and approximately 115 agents, located in a custom-built building on Castro Valley Boulevard. There were 50 parking spaces in the private lot. Tim Febig was the broker.

It was here that I met Nate Brooks, Sr., a legendary sales and business coach. Nate was physically and mentally strong with a robust personality. His proactive can-do attitude taught me how to stay focused and maintain resilience when navigating complex real estate transactions and life in general. Nate consistently reminded me that "success has a price; you either pay it now or pay it later."

This training led me to become more persistent in my approach to the day-to-day activities of the real estate business. I learned to set bigger goals for myself, invested in Craig Proctor coaching, and began to scale my business.

My accomplishments while at RE/MAX In Motion included Listing Agent of the Month, ranking in the top 10 percent of over 11,000 Sales Associates in our region of Northern California and Hawaii, and being accepted into the President's Club.

One of the most important lessons I've learned in my career is this: there is always more to learn. I love new challenges, and training others is one way to continue my quest for knowledge — to grow toward becoming the best version of myself while helping others do the same.

My 30-plus years of real estate journey have strengthened my resolve to succeed. At times, I've faltered, failed, been discounted, and counted out. I almost lost my real estate license twice regarding a latent child support issue. But through it all, I continued to show up and deliver on my promises. I chose to succeed. This level of success would not have been possible without the self-confidence and work ethic instilled in me during my upbringing, and the coaching I received while at RE/MAX and Keller Williams Realty.

SHIFTS HAPPEN

In the spring of 2005, a friend and I began looking for a property with upside potential as an investment. Our search led us to a home on Cherrybrook Commons in a small subdivision of 20 homes in San Leandro, California. The builder offered the four-bedroom, three-bath home for $680,000. A year after we moved in, the value increased to nearly $750,000.

We were on a roll and planned to buy a second investment property. Then, in December of 2007, the market shifted and sales began to slow down. In 2008, the real estate housing market crashed. We were headed for a devastating downturn. My sales plummeted.

This was the beginning of the Great Recession. It hit me like a tsunami. The Cherrybrook property was $240,000 underwater. I first listed the house for sale at $650,000, but got no offers. Two homes in the subdivision went into foreclosure and were sold for $350,000 each. After being listed multiple times, Cherrybrook eventually sold in a short sale for $436,500.

THE GREAT RECESSION OF 2007

This was the beginning of some very challenging times for me. The Great Recession sent shockwaves throughout the U.S. economy and my business. RE/MAX In Motion closed its doors and sold the building. I began questioning my decisions, doubting my abilities, and wondering if I should get out of the real estate business.

I found myself in the valley of despair. Negative thinking, self-doubt, and limiting beliefs crept into my consciousness. But by faith, grit, and perseverance, I survived.

Although the recession ended officially in 2011, my business remained sluggish, as did the businesses of many of my colleagues for several more years. I struggled to pay my bills on time and keep the utilities on. AC Transit, the local bus service, and Uber became my primary modes of transportation, because my BMW registration had expired.

It took another five years before I would fully recover and get back in the game. I was between brokerages, uncertain about my future, and living in shared subsidized housing in Alameda, California. Finally, I saved up enough money and, with the help of Swords to Plowshares, a Bay Area-based non-profit organization dedicated to helping veterans, moved into a little cottage behind my aunt's house in North Oakland.

MY AHA MOMENT

One afternoon, I sat on the couch, which was actually a loveseat since the place was not big enough for a real couch, staring at the floor. I pondered my situation and began calculating my next move. After some deep thinking, prayer, and meditation, the words of David, the Psalmist, came to mind: David said, "I will lift my eyes unto the hills." Then he asked himself a question: "Where does my help come from?"

Have you ever asked a question and, as soon as you hear your question come out of your mouth, the answer comes to you? That's what happened to David. He answered his question. And he answered mine as well: "My help comes from the Lord!"

With that revelation, I contacted the local Keller Williams Real Estate office and made an appointment with the broker the next day. I had to swallow my pride to make that call. You see, I had worked under the RE/MAX brand for 20 years. Keller Williams was a top competitor. Nevertheless, I joined the office the following day.

The broker gave me a copy of the book titled "The Millionaire Real Estate Agent" by Gary Keller. Subtitled "It's not about the money; it's about being the best you can be." Reading this book and joining Keller Williams Realty was a game-changer for me. Here, I completed Keller Williams's signature coaching program known as BOLD: Business Objective: a Life by Design.

I've been through the valley of limiting beliefs, the furnace of self-doubt, and heard the whispers of negative self-talk. Sometimes in the pursuit of our big Why, problems can seem insurmountable. I felt stuck. I was focused on my issues and viewed my situation through the lens of my recent experiences.

When we find ourselves facing what appear to be insurmountable challenges, remember we always have a choice of on which past experiences we focus. With awareness and intention, I chose to focus on the positive experiences and successes I'd had in the past. I used positive affirmations to replace negative thinking. I visualized myself back on the mountaintop. This process created a new mindset, new habits and beliefs, new behaviors, and a new self-image that aligned with the person I wanted to be. Confronting my fears transformed my inner critic into my inner coach.

Then, I took action.

Knowing who we are and what values guide and inspire us, our inner coach, or inner voice, counsels us like a wise friend. When we heed this "wise friend's" counsel, we affirm our self-worth and elevate our self-esteem. When we solve our difficulties by looking within ourselves, we learn to use the challenges we encounter as opportunities to grow, to understand our feelings and beliefs, and to discover the wisdom we have within us.

My journey has taught me how to listen to that still voice within, which reveals the lessons I need to learn and how to use my challenges as opportunities to develop a closer relationship with God.

Officially, the recession that started in December 2007 **technically** ended in the second quarter of 2011. The stock market and other economic indicators didn't fully recover until 2016. One reason for the slow economic recovery is that households and financial institutions were deeply in debt, accumulated in the years before the housing bubble burst.

I drew strength from the work ethic and mental toughness I'd developed from surviving previous downturns in the real estate market. I am a victor.

THE VALUE OF RELATIONSHIPS AND HELPING OTHERS

Whether we are realtors, coaches, trainers, or instructors, we as agents prioritize the welfare of others, sometimes at the expense of our own livelihood. This requires a high level of dedication, integrity, and compassion. We help families build generational wealth and stabilize communities through home ownership. And we add genuine value to our lives in the process.

Helping clients fulfill their dream of home ownership or helping a coaching client succeed in achieving peak performance in their life and career aligns with my values, warms my heart, and contributes to my sense of purpose. I love what I do. For over three decades, I've been party to hundreds of real estate transactions, expo-nentially and positively impacting the lives of thousands. I share a few of them in this book.

During my career as a Realtor, broker, instructor, trainer, and coach, I've had the privilege of working with some incredible clients ranging from students to renters, and first-time homebuyers to move-up buyers, empty nesters, downsizers, and millionaires buying investment proper-ties. They came from various walks of life—various colors, creeds, religions, sexual orientations, ethnicities, and socio-economic strata—who employed my services.

Some of them have become excellent sources for new business, and others have become great friends.

Relationship marketing and sphere of influence have consistently been my main source of business through the years. Staying in contact with past clients, who sometimes become friends, and colleagues pays good dividends.

One afternoon, while driving through a North Oakland neighborhood, I decided to drop in on a friend from my college days at Prairie View A&M University. He owned a soul food restaurant with two apartments above the business. We hadn't seen each other for several years.

After catching up on the happenings since we last saw each other and answering his questions regarding the state of the real estate market, he shared with me that he owned a rental property where the tenant was in the process of moving out, and he wanted to sell. It was a cosmetic fixer-upper located in the Lower Piedmont neighborhood of Oakland.

I listed the three-bedroom, two-bath, split-level home with a finished basement for $535,000 in 2014. It sold for $535,000 to a first-time buyer.

After the sale of the rental property, the seller informed me that he was ready to retire from the restaurant business and wanted to put the two-story building, consisting of a restaurant, a sports bar, and the two residential units above, on the market for sale.

I listed the property for $1,200,000. This was a complex transaction involving a mixed-use property and a liquor license. It involved extensive negotiations with the City of Oakland's planning department, the local Neighborhood Watch Group, and the Bureau of Alcohol, Tobacco, and Firearms (ATF).

A local business owner in the neighborhood noticed the For Sale sign and called me. After viewing the property, he and his agent made an offer to purchase. Recognizing the complexity of the transaction, I reached out to a commercial broker who specializes in the sale of restaurants to advise and coach me and the buyer's agent through the sales process.

The transaction was complex and exceptionally challenging. It sold in early 2015 for $1,000,000. The buyer who purchased the restaurant and sports bar referred me to his friend, who wanted to sell a restaurant business she owned in Alameda, California.

Building and nurturing relationships is a pleasant and sustainable way to scale your business. Relationships matter not only in sales between agents and clients but also between coach and client.

I've learned valuable lessons from each market shift. One is whether the market is up or down; you should be mindful of daily sales data, such as the number of new listings, the number of homes sold, and days on the market. These stats are invaluable for recognizing the nuanced changes in the real estate market, whether we're in a balanced market, a buyers' market, or a sellers' market.

As agents, our livelihood is derived from monetizing our knowledge and expertise, and our time, but our main product is, or should be, service. We provide the best service when we are knowledgeable. Well-informed, well-trained agents should aim to become knowledge brokers.

Part of an agent's daily routine and preparation should be to follow current events and peruse MLS statistical data for significant changes. When there is a shift in the housing market, it is usually caused by events that erode public confidence and optimism related to economic, political, or ecological events (think 9/11, the housing bubble and burst of 2008, and the COVID-19 pandemic of 2020).

Use available resources to stay informed about the market in your area. Your local Multiple Listing Service maintains statistical data that includes current and year-over-year numbers for "Quantity Sold," "Volume Sold," "Average Sale," "Median Sale," and "Quantity Active."

Also, know your numbers. What numbers do you need to hit to reach your goals and maintain your projected gross commission income? In a declining market, these numbers will need to be adjusted upward. You'll also need to increase the number of hours you work per day to maintain the same amount of gross commission income.

Shifts affect different market areas differently. All neighborhoods are not affected the same in a declining or rising real estate market.

My emphasis here is on how to survive downward shifts in the real estate market. The reason is that it's easier to stay in business and make money in a hot market. It's during the hot markets that lots of new agents enter the real estate business. Downward market shifts separate winners from the rest of the pack.

Stay focused on the four key activities that lead to success: Daily Preparation, Daily Lead Generation, Setting Appointments, and Closing Escrows. These activities should always be aligned with your values and contribute to your sense of purpose.

Success is not only measured by how many homes you sell or how much money you make, but rather by finding fulfillment and purpose in these activities and the outcomes they produce. Then you will discover success, happiness, and significance. Significance is when you help others achieve goals that they previously thought were out of reach. This is where I find my greatest joy. This is the fruit of my labor.

EXPERIENCE IS THE BEST TEACHER

I share my experiences and professional observations here so agents, especially new agents, will learn to enjoy the boom times **and** prepare for future market shifts, which will come about at some point during their career.

This information is a simplified overview of what agents do to survive in down markets. I hope it can be used as a guide for agents working in the real estate business. I discuss agents' daily activities in more detail in the chapter on coaching. I dive deeply into these topics in my workshops.

Secondly, and perhaps more to my point, the housing market has gone through up-and-down cycles for as long as we've been keeping records. Bubbles come and go. Nevertheless, no matter how often or how seldom cycles occur, it is extremely challenging and nearly impossible to pinpoint the timing when a declining market hits bottom.

Lots of emphasis is placed here on down markets because they present the greatest external challenge most agents will face in their real estate career.

Although market shifts are out of our control, we can manage that which is within our control: our attitude, our efforts, and our beliefs.

Secondly, we must avoid the negative narratives about the market's poor state. Do not join the "Ain't It Awful" club. Stay focused, set big goals, survive, and thrive. That's what I did. And you can do it too.

SURVIVING AND THRIVING AMID ECONOMIC DOWNTURNS

The following is a list of activities that helped me navigate challenging events in my life. I offer these activities as a guide for those who choose to follow them.

- Prayer and meditation are good habits to continue and reinforce if necessary to help you through this season of challenges in your life. Exercise, eat healthy foods, and get plenty of rest and sleep. Renew your strength and faith.

- Maintain your sense of purpose and stay focused on your big Why. Maintain alignment of your activities with your core values and beliefs. Keep the flame burning under your passions and desires.
- If you've been following me for a while, you know I believe all successful people begin their day with a well-organized routine. My routine is based on a method called S.A.V.E.R.S. from the book Miracle Morning by Hal Elrod. It consists of Silence, Affirmations, Visualization, Exercise, Reading, and Scribing. This is how I spend the first hour of my day when time permits. There are days when I spend 1 minute on each of these practices. No matter how chaotic things around you may become, stick to your morning routine. It keeps you grounded and enjoying a sense of security through consistency and affirmations.
- Stay in close contact with friends and family members who are supportive. Avoid negative energy.
- Anxiety feeds on analysis paralysis. Remember, you have choices. Exercise the choices you have. Taking action will help you regain momentum, which in turn builds confidence and opens up new possibilities.

- Acknowledge and celebrate your wins, no matter how small. When you celebrate your victories and express gratitude for them, your brain releases dopamine, a chemical messenger that stimulates motivation and boosts your confidence. This is the payoff for the action you've taken. Your increasing confidence adds to your desire for more wins.

TIMING THE MARKET IS DIFFICULT

There is an adage that says "time *in the market* is better than *timing the market.*" Some clients will tell you they want to wait until the market hits bottom before they buy. Or they will want to wait until the market peaks before they sell. Timing the market is exceedingly challenging. The only way we know when a down market has hit absolute bottom is when it starts moving back up.

So, how do we prepare for the change, whether it's an increase or a decrease? Know your market. Be vigilant and keep current with the changes in the market activity.

Lead generation becomes more crucial and selective. Set yourself apart from the crowd. The best way to set yourself apart is to be authentic. Be the best version of yourself. Use the resources available to you through education, training, and coaching. One of the traits of success is "willingness to learn." Cultivate a growth mindset. Knowledge is power.

Whether the market is up or down, a situation to be careful of and avoid is transactions that look great at the onset but may be problematic in the details.

As real estate professionals, we're always eager to help a client with their real estate needs. In our desire to help the client, we sometimes look past the initial "red flags" and see opportunity. But the sooner you realize some problems are most likely insurmountable, don't hesitate to inform your client and reach an agreement to cancel the contract.

Here's an example: My teammate Kim Cleghorn and I took a listing on a West Oakland duplex in the spring of 2022. The list price was a million dollars.

The situation was this: The owner had subdivided one of four properties situated on one lot into a two-unit condominium. Our due diligence found that the Alameda County Planning Department had granted the subdivision, but the tax office had not yet issued separate parcel numbers for the subdivided property. The seller told us the parcel numbers were forthcoming and he should have them any day.

With the listing agreement signed and the parcel numbers "forthcoming," the seller pressed us hard to put the property on the MLS and begin marketing it immediately.

We could have entered the property on the MLS under the original parcel number, found a buyer, and gotten paid. However, our experience told us that it could become problematic for the buyer and, consequently, for us as agents. The fact that the property record did not reflect the new parcel number for the newly created subdivision was a "red flag."

We consulted our legal department for guidance and recommendations. We explained the options the seller offered. The attorney advised us to cancel the listing, which we did with the seller's reluctant agreement.

We could have entered the listing on the MLS under the original parcel number, found a buyer for the property, and, assuming the title company didn't catch the issue, collected nearly a $50,000 commission check. Whether the title company caught it or not, this was a lawsuit waiting to happen. We avoided a big problem by focusing on the client and not the commission.

We only truly know the market has hit bottom when it starts to go back up. By this time, we've missed the absolute bottom. The same is true for a red-hot real estate market. We know the market has peaked when it starts to trend downward.

Whether the market is up or down, some agents consistently achieve their goals and thrive. These are the top producers. In a down market, you will have clients who will tell you they want to wait until the market hits bottom before they buy. Or in an upmarket, they will think the crazy hot market will continue going up. They want to wait until they can sell for a higher price. I caution any buyer or seller not to base their decision on waiting to sell for more money, attempting to time the market. I'm often asked, "When is a good time to buy?" My answer is always the same:

"When you find the house you like, and the monthly payments fit your budget, it's time to buy."

MY RELATIONSHIP WITH MY FRIEND AND COLLEAGUE PAYS OFF

Since I transitioned into training and coaching, I've continued to serve buyers and sellers in my sphere of influence, past clients, and referrals. In the summer of 2022, a former client contacted me and asked me to find a house for their daughter, Megan, to purchase.

A colleague of mine, Eddie Walker, keeps me updated on any new properties he's listing. So when Megan's parents asked me to find her a property, I remembered a beautiful, well-priced home in the lower Oakland Hills that had just been listed. I showed the property to Megan. She liked it and made an offer that Eddie's sellers accepted.

Having transitioned into training and coaching, and being out of sync with new office policies and procedures, our KW Team Leader insisted I team up with another agent in the office to complete a buyer transaction I had initiated. I did so with outstanding results.

During January 2022, my teammate and I had over two million dollars of transactions: We had in escrow Megan, a first-time buyer at a $735,000 property in East Oakland hills; Kelly, a first-time buyer in escrow to purchase a duplex in Sacramento for over $419,000, and Philip, the seller in West Oakland, with a list price of $1 million. This was a good month!

Since 1990, I've been blessed to help families, businesses, investors, and single individuals buy and sell real estate from San Leandro in the East Bay to San Anselmo in the West Bay and just about every city in between, including San Francisco. I'm sharing some of the most memorable ones here as examples of the business of representing buyers and sellers and some of the challenges that come along with the profession.

The joy of handing someone the keys to the largest investment of a lifetime and saying "Thank You, Congratulations!" is priceless. I sold a young couple their first home in Richmond, California, in the mid-1990s. When I met them at the house to give them the keys, the wife was so excited she asked me to carry her over the threshold, which I did. It was hilarious! Once we were inside, her husband insisted that he and I smoke Cuban cigars. This was an unforgettable transaction.

Buyers are always super excited when escrow closes. This is not always the case with sellers. I remember a seller who contracted with me to sell his home in Berkeley in the early 2000s. Based on the comparative market analysis that I completed for him, he had approximately $200,000 in equity in the house. He had purchased the home about three years earlier. He was born and raised in Syria. He told me the story of how he'd come to this country with very little money. He managed to buy a used Lincoln Continental and got a license to operate it as a taxi. Eventually, he was operating four additional cabs and drivers.

After a month on the market, I brought a buyer who made a full price offer. This was the buyer's first home.

She was excited because it was only a few blocks from her dad's home. The buyer signed all escrow documents and was ready to close. All we needed was the seller's signature. With all contingencies released, the seller and I met at the title company, where the escrow officer walked us through the closing statement as is customary. (This was before the TILA-RESPA Integrated Disclosure in 2015) in our area at the time.

Based on the Seller's Closing Statement, he was netting $197,000 and some change. The seller looked at me and said, "I thought you told me I was getting $200,000 from this sale." I said, "Yes, but..." I thought he was simply pointing out a fact. However, the seller put down the pen, stood up, and walked out of the title company. He didn't even want to negotiate with me or the seller. The deal fell apart.

Point to remember: The seller, along with the agent, establishes the list price for the property. However, it's the buyer who sets the actual sales price based on their willingness to pay for the property, regardless of the seller's asking price. This business is not for the faint of heart.

Despite the challenges and vicissitudes of the real estate business, the opportunity to represent buyers and sellers in the largest investment most people will ever make is a worthy occupation.

THE LAW OF ATTRACTION

By the time the COVID-19 pandemic disrupted life as we know it and upset the residential real estate market, I had already begun using the knowledge and experience I'd accumulated over the past two and a half decades to expand my business into real estate education.

In 2017, I was offered a part-time position with a private real estate school as an instructor for real estate pre-licensing courses. At the time, the school was operating three campuses: Vallejo, Concord, and San Francisco. On a leap of faith, I stepped out of my comfort zone and committed to teaching Real Estate Principles, Real Estate Law, and Real Estate Practice in twelve-week intervals on Saturday mornings. I taught these courses for two and a half years.

A few months later, I received a call from Guy Forkner, Co-Chair of the real estate department at Merritt College in Oakland, California. He had viewed my profile on LinkedIn. He invited me to become a guest lecturer for his Real Estate Practice class of approximately 60 students. His students were very studious and attentive.

Among the many questions they asked was what my largest commission check was. I shared the transaction where I sold the restaurant and sports bar with two apartments upstairs, which sold for one million dollars at a 5 percent commission. They found the details of that transaction fascinating. It fueled their excitement for the course and the possibility of becoming licensed agents.

The last line in Guy Forkner's introduction of me was "Roy is a survivor!" This line provided a segue for me to talk about how to survive the liabilities, challenges, and risks involved in the real estate business, and the fact that most agents drop out of the business in their first year. By year five, the turnover rate is eighty-seven percent.

I enjoyed lecturing at Merritt. I even received a referral for a listing from one of the students. I was super excited when Mr. Forkner invited me back to lecture another class the following semester. Mr. Forkner was right: I am a survivor. Little did I know that I was going to have to pull out all my survival skills for what was to come next.

THE 2020 PANDEMIC DRAMATICALLY CHANGED THE REAL ESTATE INDUSTRY

The COVID-19 pandemic sent shockwaves through the real estate housing market and the way agents work. Sales dropped to their lowest levels since the financial crisis in 2007. This dramatic drop occurred in home sales, not home prices. Some sellers were reluctant to put their homes on the market for fear that no one would view them, and they would sit unsold.

Consequently, new listings dropped by about 40 percent from the previous year. Buyers held off on purchasing their next home. Business closures and job losses took a toll on the economy. By April 2020, unemployment was 14 percent. We were in a COVID-19 recession.

The question my clients were asking was whether this was a repeat of the housing crisis of 2007, which was still etched in their memory. The answer was "No." And, of course, time validated this response.

Aggressive government stimulus programs and extended unemployment benefits bolstered household incomes. This helped keep the demand for housing virtually unchanged. These two factors, coupled with historically low interest rates and the increased need to work from home, accelerated demand for housing and began to push prices higher.

By September of 2021, home-buying activity had reached pre-pandemic levels. Historically low interest rates, remote working, and new buyer needs like social distancing, home offices, and space for home schooling brought buyers back into the market full force.

The pandemic reshaped buyers' buying patterns. No longer concerned about commuting, they were free to live further away from the workplace, oftentimes moving to larger homes in areas where prices were more affordable.

Real estate, as I had known it for nearly thirty years, changed dramatically on March 4, 2020, when Governor Gavin Newsom issued Executive Order N-33-20 proclaiming "a State of Emergency to exist in California as a result of the threat of COVID-19."

The COVID-19 pandemic ushered in a new paradigm for the real estate housing market, changing the way homes were listed, marketed, and viewed. Real estate offices were off-limits, and all in-person meetings were suspended.

Changes were not limited to California, where I work. Agents all across the country had to rethink every aspect of the real estate business. In my market area, open houses were suspended for months. Listing presentations with sellers, buyer viewings, presenting offers, walk-throughs, and escrow closings were done virtually.

Social media marketing and virtual tours became neces-sary. Once open houses resumed, masks, gloves, booties, hand sanitizer, and sanitary wipes were mandatory at every open house. Social distancing was strictly enforced. The only multiple viewers allowed in the property at the same time were members of the same family.

Viewers were not allowed to touch anything in the house. The agent had to wipe down all railings, doorknobs, toilets, and any other surfaces a viewer may have touched before the next individual or family could enter.

FROM SURVIVING TO THRIVING IN THE COVID-19 REAL ESTATE MARKET

Many agents not only survived but thrived in the pandemic-induced recession. Miracle Holt, a Realtor in Atlanta, Georgia, built a thriving business during the COVID-19 health crisis. When asked how she did it, she said she focused on her strengths, outsourced non-essential tasks, and created a "showing partner position" to leverage her time to focus on growing her business. She also let go of some relationships that did not have her best interests at heart.

Another agent, Nichole Jones, said she nurtured friendships, prioritized interactions with social distancing, and relied on her network of friends and contacts to leverage sales that led to one of the most successful periods of her career.

In April of 2020, two months after the coronavirus shut down most of the world, I listed a condominium for sale located at 1388 Jacqueline Place in San Lorenzo, California. The list price was $539,000. It was the only listing I had on the market at that time, so I was able to focus a lot of time and energy on my network of friends and team members to get the unit sold. COVID-19 protocols notwithstanding, the property sold in 24 days for $539,800.

A seismic shift occurred in the residential real estate market. The pandemic ushered in a new paradigm for the real estate industry. The technological changes that were happening before the pandemic accelerated.

It changed the way homes are listed, marketed, and viewed, and where buyers are purchasing homes. The pandemic has changed the nature of home and work. Buyers are no longer tied to a particular location with the daily commute in mind. Greater emphasis is placed on characteristics in a house that are conducive to remote work and homeschooling rather than community amenities.

What enabled me to use my survival skills to make this sale happen? Two words: persistence and mastery. But these didn't come easily. I've learned both skills through surviving four economic downturns in my career and through various roles across multiple industries.

I sincerely believe my successes in helping others succeed not only in real estate but also in other professional disciplines as well is the result of the journey my life has taken—from a farm in Texas to a career in Bay Area tech, to the vibrant, ever-changing, and ever-exciting realm of real estate, and now training and coaching.

Moving from Information Technology to real estate was made with the realization that the tech industry was advancing at breakneck speed. Technology had finally made its way into real estate. It wouldn't be long before technology would dominate the real estate industry and become an indispensable tool in every aspect of the business.

It was now incumbent upon me to prepare myself for what was coming down the pike. My life has been an exciting journey of preparation, challenges, and opportunities. Let me tell you how I got here.

Chapter 6
Finding My Niche

I will speak your statutes before kings, and I will not be put to shame.

— Psalm 119:46

ROUTE 66 AND BACK TO CALIFORNIA

Having survived 18 months of living day to day in a combat zone and the military draft that interrupted my life back in October 1967, I wanted to get on with taking charge of my life. The year was 1970. My dad wanted me to settle down in Texas. But most of my friends had moved away. The ones remaining had gotten married and started families. Opportunities were limited. King Cotton was dead. I didn't see a future for me in Chappell Hill. And I didn't want to go back to PVAMU.

My brother Travis and I left Austin, Texas, in August 1970, taking turns driving my Ford Mustang back to California. We connected with the historic U.S. Highway Route 66 in Glenrio, Texas, near the New Mexico border. This took us to Bakersfield and from there to Berkeley. There was both symbolism and history in this route. The historic highway was used by travelers in the 1930s who migrated from the South, full of faith and hope, in search of new beginnings. I was on a journey to new opportunities.

THE EMERGING POWER OF COMPUTERS WAS TOP OF MIND FOR ME WHEN I RETURNED HOME

The power of computers was evident in Vietnam. The Vietnam War was the first war in military history to rely heavily on computers. As a personnel specialist with a secret security clearance, my MOS provided me with the knowledge that computers played a significant role in dictating troop activities on the battlefield and extended to the office of the President of the United States.

I'd grown accustomed to the high-powered, intense, and impactful training provided in the Military. To return to

PVAMU at that time seemed like a step back in time. This realization prompted me to use the GI Bill to enroll in the Academy of Computer Technology in Downtown San Francisco in September 1970. The Academy at that time provided training in two computer Languages: Report Program Generator (RPG), a high-level programming language for business applications. It was used primarily on IBM's operating system. The other language taught at the Academy was COBOL (Common Business Oriented Language.) Having completed this training, I landed a job as a computer programmer with the City of Berkeley.

In addition, I had fallen in love with the San Francisco Bay Area when I visited my uncle Gussie in 1967. After visiting my parents, immediate family, friends, and other relatives in Chappell Hill, I decided to put down roots in California. With California on my mind, I purchased a 1966 Ford Mustang convertible, planning to return to Berkeley.

A lot had changed in the two and a half years I'd been in the Army. Richard Nixon was now the president of the United States. The nation was bitterly divided over the direction of the Vietnam War. The Civil Rights Act of 1968 was signed into law by President Lyndon Johnson. Fair Housing was the law of the land. My three brothers, Travis, Lawrence, and Melvin, had also joined the US

Army National Guard. My sister Madelyn was at Pan American University in the Rio Grande Valley.

MAKING A HOME IN BERKELEY

I settled in Berkeley on Ashby Avenue, a few blocks from my Uncle Gussie. My old roommate from PVAMU, Stelton Mitchell, was looking for a roommate and invited me to share his two-bedroom apartment. Stelton was a teacher and coach at Berkeley High School. Using the GI Bill, I enrolled in the Academy of Computer Technology in San Francisco.

Six months later, I earned a certificate in computer programming and landed a job with the City of Berkeley as a programmer on a federal grant program. Under the supervision of Jim Thompson, the Data Processing manager, I worked alongside a senior programmer analyst to automate the human resources personnel records. The conversion also included the City's parking citation records. I gained valuable analytical skills in the process.

Pollie (Paula) Pate lived in the same apartment building in South Berkeley. One evening, while pulling into her assigned parking space, which was next to mine, she side-swiped the rear quarter panel of my car. Yes, the red Mustang convertible. She left a note on my car, instructing me to call her, and she would take care of the damage. That began a 30-year relationship. She was a single mother with four kids. Two years later, we were parenting a family of five.

Our son, Malcolm, was born on March 4, 1972, at Alta Bates Hospital, where she worked as a nurse. When we learned she was pregnant, we began searching for a house to buy in North Berkeley. The agents we contacted told us that "They" would never sell a North Berkeley home to a Black family. I've always believed that I'm divinely guided and protected and that things always work out for me. Paula contacted real estate broker Earl Grindsted of Vernon Morris Real Estate, a Black owned brokerage in South Berkeley. Mr. Grindsted, through his connections and extensive experience, delivered on his promise. When Malcolm was born, we brought him home to 1348 Neilson Street in North Berkeley, where he joined his siblings Broma, Tony, Eddie, and Sacratine.

Paula worked the 11 P.M. to 7 A.M. shift at Alta Bates Hospital so she could be home with the baby during the day. I would get home around 5:30 in the evening in time for dinner and family time. This system worked for 5 years, when Paula and I decided to live separately. It continued to work for the next 25 years.

After working for 2 years at the City of Berkeley, I used my GI Bill, which required no down payment, to purchase a duplex in East Oakland, which tenants then occupied. President Richard Nixon ended the grant program under which I was employed at the City of Berkeley in 1974. I found myself unemployed and looking for a new job.

By attending night classes at Laney College, which were free during the 1970s, the monthly educational benefits from the GI Bill were a blessing. It, along with Paula's income and the cash flow from the duplex, allowed us to pay the bills, keep the kids fed and clothed, and keep them in school. By the grace of God, we persevered until I found my next job.

DIALING FOR DOLLARS

Dialing for Dollars was a television show where the host gave out a password at the start of the show and then showed a movie. During commercial breaks, the host would make a random telephone call from a batch of phone numbers mailed in by viewers. I entered my number. If the viewer knew the answer, the winners received money and other prizes. I used to watch the franchised version of the show in the late 1970s. One afternoon, as I sat watching the show, the host dialed a random number as usual, and after a brief pause, my phone rang! I could hardly contain my excitement since I knew the password for the day.

When I answered the phone, it was not Dialing for Dollars on the other end of the line; it was Bank of America calling to tell me that they had reviewed my resume and wanted me to come in for an interview the next day. I'd won the *resume* contest. The bank hired me as a Systems Analyst in their small systems data processing department. Small in the sense that we worked with IBM System/360 series instead of IBM System/370 Mainframes. The valuable skills I had learned at the City of Berkeley, analyzing and converting manual systems to fully automated systems, paid good dividends.

WORKING AT A BANK OF AMERICA DATA PROCESSING CENTER

National and international wire transfers at Bank of America were processed manually until late 1978. The remittance accounting department utilized a team of data entry key punch operators to enter wire transfer requests using IBM punched cards, which were then fed into an IBM System/360 computer. These computer-generated reports detail all wire transactions, including short-term loans made by Bank of America to other banks locally and worldwide. In the manual system, turnaround time was slow. Turnaround time was slow when tracking time-sensitive transactions. This included monitoring when funds were due to be received from other banks, including the amounts owed and interest.

This was a herculean task to manage manually. And even more challenging was reconciling and managing the process of short-term loans to other banks. The manual computer system in place used a series of stand-alone programs that were driven by transferring information entered on IBM punched cards.

The actual wire transfers were completed using Western Union telegrams. Our team, the Remittance Accounting Project (RAP), was named after the Remittance Accounting Procedures department. Our 8-member team, which included David Pugh, a consultant from IBM, designed, developed, wrote computer code, tested, and implemented a fully automated remittance accounting system in 18 months. The system processed over $500 million a day.

The resistance and pushback to automation in 1978 were extraordinary. The remittance accounting department at Bank of America was the most lucrative in the bank. We had meetings with the highest echelons of the department to share and defend our design and plans for implementation. I had developed a decision table comparing the automated system we designed to the existing manual system. To develop the decision table, I posed various questions with weighted values to determine the advantages of the new proposed system. We were getting bombarded with questions and criticism based on assumptions management had made about the shortcomings of a fully automated system.

During the first meeting, our team was being dominated by the opposition, who openly expressed their concerns and criticisms of the automated system. Our project manager, Jim George, listened but did not respond to their problems, as we programmers had already addressed them in our code solutions. Perhaps because he had no computer programming experience and needed to meet with us before responding, it felt like the system we had so painstakingly designed was headed for defeat. Much to the chagrin of the project manager and others in the room, I started responding to their comments, sometimes out of turn. Afterward, at our usual Happy Hour bar, located around the corner from the office, I overheard one of the mid-level managers criticizing me for speaking out of turn during the meeting.

One of the pressing questions upper management had was how to replicate the verification process in the automated system. In the manual system, documents requesting a wire transfer were assigned to a keypunch operator. The operator entered the data. The output was a card file that was then assigned to a verification operator using the punch card file as input. The verification process worked much like re-entering our email address to ensure it matches the one we provided.

The code I wrote for the wire transfer verification program allowed the operator to enter the data online. The data entry program created two identical electronic output files: a master file and a verification file. When the verification operator logged on to verify the transactions, the data entry program used the verification file as input. Each time the verification operator entered a keystroke, it was compared to what had been entered previously into the master file. Any errors and mismatched transactions were printed out for manual verification. It was a masterful design, although the project manager never acknowledged it.

When we made our final presentation for approval, there were over a dozen top-level managers present, including their assistants and mid-level managers. We had to convince them that the new system was foolproof and our code was secure and accurate enough to handle the approximately $500 million that passed through the system daily. Accuracy was paramount. Our team prevailed. The automated system was accepted.

I was let go, along with two other team members, after we implemented the automated system. Three of us went on to do contract programming work. My participation in the Remittance Accounting Project (RAP) launched my nearly 18-year career as a systems analyst and computer programmer. Twelve of those years, I worked as an independent contractor.

Computer conversion projects are the most challenging and the most rewarding for a programmer/analyst. Conversions and upgrades are necessary to keep companies competitive and profitable. Conversions require detailed analysis, creativity, and good coding skills. After the RAP project at Bank of America, my next total system conversion project was with Golden Grain Macaroni Company in San Leandro, California, in 1980. In addition to the conversion, all the computer programs used by Ghirardelli Chocolate, which Golden Grain Macaroni Company then owned, were written in the COBOL programming language. Since I was the only programmer trained in the language, it was my responsibility to modify those programs to be compatible with the newly converted system.

MY DAD, BROTHER, AND HIS FAMILY VISITED ME IN UNION CITY, CALIFORNIA

This was Travis's third trip to California and my dad's first. I was happy to see them. It was a very special occasion for my dad. I took him to see Gussie, whom he had not seen since Gussie's visit to Chappell Hill in the 1950s. It was a happy occasion.

The year was 1980. I was still working at Golden Grain Macaroni Company. Paula (Pollie) and I had grown apart and gone our separate ways, although we maintained the family ties that bound us together, albeit separately, for the next 25 years. My 8-year-old son Malcolm was now living with me. In the Fall of 1982, I answered an ad placed by a silicon wafer manufacturing company in Marin County for a programmer/analyst. I accepted the contract and moved to Fairfax, California.

Malcolm was a 4th grader when I enrolled him in White Hill Elementary School, where he made the soccer team as a Forward. After graduating from White Hill, he attended Marin Catholic High School, where he played baseball and football. Despite his small size, he held the position of wide receiver on the football team. He caught a touchdown pass in the closing minutes to win the game and the championship for the Marin Catholic Wildcats in 1988.

GROWING IN SERVICE TO MY COMMUNITY

Moving to Marin County marked the beginning of a new chapter in my purpose-driven life. Concerned Parents of Novato (CPON) is a nonprofit organization dedicated to enhancing the community of Novato by offering cultural enrichment, tutoring, academic scholarships, and community service opportunities for its youth. The organization was founded in 1982 by a group of prominent African American families who wanted to network with other Novato families through civic, cultural, charitable, and educational opportunities. When one of the group's members reached out to me to join, I gladly accepted.

Through CPON, I met my now long-time friend, Otis Bruce, a recent graduate of Hastings Law School in San Francisco. Otis introduced me to the Democratic Central Committee of Marin. The DCCM is the official representative of the Democratic Party in Marin County. In 1988, Otis and I were selected to be delegates to the state convention in Sacramento for presidential candidate Bill Clinton. At the convention, Otis and I had the honor of meeting the esteemed civil rights activist Rosa Parks. I took a photo of her and Otis together on the convention floor.

Meeting Mrs. Rosa Parks in person was an awe-inspiring experience. She was, and still is, a civil rights icon. Her

153

refusal to give up her seat, in a section of the bus reserved for "Whites" to a white man, and move to the back of the bus sparked one of the most successful boycotts of the civil rights movement. She was arrested and jailed for taking a stand against segregation. Her arrest led to a 381-day boycott of the Montgomery, Alabama, bus company. The bus company conceded defeat, which eventually led to the Supreme Court decision to ban segregation on public transportation in 1956. She demonstrated how the power of one individual can effect change for the greater good.

In 1994, Jackie Wright, a director with the Marin County Chapter of the American Red Cross, reached out and invited me to join the board. I accepted the position and served on the Marin County board for almost 4 years. This marked the beginning of a long-standing relationship with the ARC, which would ultimately lead to significant accomplishments for both me and the ARC youth. Each summer, I helped lead the Leadership Development Camp (LDC). LDC is designed for youth between the ages of 13 and 18 and aims to develop leadership skills, public speaking abilities, diversity awareness, and teamwork.

Working with youth at LDC also helped me hone my leadership and training skills. Our goal at ARC was to help the participants discover their unique talents and grow into leaders within the Red Cross and in their academic and personal lives. Our goal at LDC was to help participants, referred to as LDC delegates, discover their unique skills and grow into leaders, both within the Red Cross and in their academic and personal lives, to make a difference in their communities, nationally, and around the world.

Attendance at LDC was a coveted recognition. Each participant in attendance was selected by their youth services coordinator for having demonstrated leadership qualities in their volunteer work with their respective chapters during the year.

Also in attendance each summer were two Chapman-Holcombe international Interns representing the International Federation of Red Cross and Red Crescent Societies (IFRC). Youth services coordinator from six Bay Area Counties, including Alameda, paid staff, parent chaperones, and any ARC volunteers who wish to visit the camp during the day. We held workshops where we discussed disaster preparedness, including mitigation, the ARC mission, and our duties and responsibilities to each other.

When I relocated to Oakland from Fairfax in Marin County in 2000, I joined the Alameda County Chapter of the American Red Cross as a member of the board of directors. The Oakland office was led by Marian Wilson-Sylvestry, who served as operations manager. As a director, one of my duties was to serve as a liaison between the board and Youth Services. After a few months in this role, I suggested that, instead of reporting to Youth Services regarding any board decisions that affect the youth and bringing their concerns and questions back to the board, we add two youths to our board.

The board agreed unanimously. This decision opened two-way communication between the board and the youth. The youth benefited, and the Youth Services Committee grew stronger and more popular as a result of having their peers communicate directly with them. The board benefited by receiving firsthand communications from them through their youth board members. It was a win-win solution for everyone involved with the youth.

The board was proud and excited when one of our youth board members, Sandy Tesch, was selected to represent the Alameda County Chapter on the Youth Services Committee at the national level in Washington, D.C. This announcement prompted Harry Hartman, my colleague on the board, to state at the subsequent monthly meeting "Roy has put the Alameda County Red Cross youth on the map."

Sandy Tesch Wilkins remains a devoted member of the ARC and has been a Youth Commission Member at the International Federation of Red Cross and Red Crescent Societies, Geneva, Switzerland, since 1911. During my second term as a director with the Alameda County Chapter, it would no longer be a separate board, but would instead become the Alameda County Leadership Council. Near the end of my second term as a member of the Leadership Council, Marian referred me to the American Red Cross Bay Area (ARCBAC) Youth Services Committee in San Francisco.

Although we only knew each other in the work environment, I considered Marian a friend and mentor. She was constantly encouraging and motivating me to grow and become more involved in the ARC. She paved the way for me to hone my leadership skills. I'm grateful for the leadership she provided. Marian was a dedicated Red Cross Leader with superb communication skills.

I met Stephen Zellerbach for the first time at my first ARCBA Youth Services Committee meeting in San Francisco. Stephen was the chairman of the committee. I found him to be a warm, cordial man of few words. ARCBA Youth Services Committee members included coordinators from six of the nine Bay Area Counties: Alameda, Contra Costa, Solano, Marin, San Francisco, and San Mateo. At that time, each county had its own youth services coordinator. As chairman, He conducted monthly meetings and addressed the needs and concerns of the coordinators.

Before leaving for vacation in Europe, he asked me to conduct the monthly meetings in his stead during his absence. When he returned, he asked me to serve as his vice chairman, and I accepted the offer. I served in this position for two years. Mr. Zellerbach was a fourth-generation San Franciscan, a businessman, a community activist, a world traveler, a gentleman, and a scholar. He was a good man to know and share the gavel with. He and his family were avid, generational volunteers and supporters of The American Red Cross.

Sometime around 2005, the youth services coordinator, Alissa May, and I organized a trip and took a group of Red Cross youth from the Oakland Chapter, including our Chapman-Holcombe International Interns, to visit Stephen at his summer home in Healdsburg, California. Our visit took place on a beautiful Fall day. The weather was warm and sunny. We all spent the entire day with him and his wife, Cecilia, along with several of their friends who had prepared an assortment of food for us.

We all hung out around the swimming pool with Stephen, eating, laughing, talking, and reminiscing about his work with the Red Cross, while the kids swam. It was a good day. To say we made their day would be an understatement. The visit overjoyed Steven. They both expressed their heartfelt gratitude for our visit as we packed up and left for Oakland in both cars.

RED CROSS YOUTH GET APPROVAL TO PARTICIPATE IN DISASTER RESPONSE

While on the Oakland Leadership Council at the urging of some of the Red Cross youth and with the help of the Alameda County disaster team leader in the Oakland Chapter, I was instrumental in working with Rita Chick, HR officer, at ARC Headquarters in San Francisco where she worked, to get final approval for our request to allow ARC youth to respond to disasters along with adult responders.

The board finally agreed with the condition that the youth could respond only at times that would not interfere with schoolwork. In our last meeting with Rita to convince her to support approval of our request, I made the salient point that during a disaster where children are present, they too are impacted and experience pain and trauma just like adults, perhaps even more. How comforting would it be for children amid a disaster to look up and see someone their age there to help and comfort them? The question piqued the awareness of enough board members to vote in favor of the proposal.

I JOINED ALLEN TEMPLE MISSIONARY BAPTIST CHURCH

My membership at Allen Temple Baptist Church began in Oakland in 1987. Before joining ATBC, I visited and worshiped at a dozen different churches in Oakland from 1975 to 1986, looking for a church that offered the unadulterated gospel that I grew up with as a member of Allwise Missionary Baptist Church in Texas.

One day, a friend at work asked me if I knew about Allen Temple. She had visited there several times and thought I might like it. I knew after my first visit that I had found my church home. I've been there ever since.

Worshipping and serving at ATBC has deepened my understanding of theology and the ministry of Jesus, which in turn has strengthened my faith and helped me grow in the knowledge that the real work of a Christian is not limited to the four walls of the church building. We can not be content going to church on Sundays and then spending the rest of the week in the "rocking chair of lazy religion."

Instead, we must put our faith into action. My faith walk at Allen Temple, under the leadership of the Reverend Doctor Jacqueline A. Thompson. Tutelage of the Reverend Doctor J. Alfred Smith, Sr. Pastor Emeritus (at the time of this writing), and his successor, Reverend Doctor J. Alfred Smith, Jr., helped me understand, at a deeper level, what it means to do justly, love mercy, and walk humbly with God. The ministry of Jesus teaches us to treat all people with dignity and respect; To help provide for the least, the lowest, and the left out.

Serving in a leadership capacity as president of the Oakland Coalition of Congregations (OCC), representing my church, fueled my passion for empowering people to act effectively in their self-interest by participating in the educational, political, environmental, social, and economic activities wherever decisions are being made by governmental powers that directly affect their lives. It is our duty as followers of Christ to speak for those who cannot, will not, or are unable to speak for themselves.

Pastor Smith's powerful, biblically based teachings implored us church leaders to *speak truth to power* long before the phrase became a cliché. When we speak truth to power, we must remain steadfast, even though there may be consequences. We must be like David the Psalmist, who asked God to "Never take your word of truth from my mouth."… David goes on to say, "I will speak your statutes before kings and I will not be put to shame." Let us remember, God did not give us a spirit of fear; he gave us a spirit of power, of love, and a sound mind.

Not all Christians feel that the church should be involved in the political arena. Some people ask, *Should the church be involved in politics?* My training under the leadership of Pastor J. Alfred Smith, Sr, requires me to answer this question in the affirmative. Scripture tells us that God is sovereign over *all* things. Politics is just another conduit God uses to carry out His will. As followers of Jesus, we must proclaim the gospel in *all* aspects of our lives, including politics.

PREPARING ALLEN TEMPLE YOUTH FOR LEADERSHIP

Sometime around 1989, if my memory serves me correctly, Pastor Smith shared his vision of rejuvenating our church by recruiting, training, and involving young people in its leadership. He called his vision "The Greening of Allen Temple." Dr. Smith's position was that church leadership would suffer and the church would begin to decline unless proactive measures were taken to train and mentor our youth for leadership. To that end, he recruited a young minister named Marcus "Goodie"

Goodloe, a native of Compton, California, to head the youth ministry at Allen Temple.

I was one of the Youth Team Leaders that Minister Goodloe assembled to assist with developing programs for the youth of Allen Temple. Under his leadership, along with a team of youth workers, we led sessions to teach biblical doctrine, conducted Bible studies, and organized workshops — as well as field trips, social outings, and spiritual renewal retreats. We created the Youth and Children's Spotlight, through which we recognized a youth and an elementary student for their outstanding achievements in academic, community, and church service. We taught the youth decorum and leadership by modeling the type of leaders we wanted them to become.

We recognized their contributions by inviting them to the stage along with their parents, where I introduced them to the congregation and shared their academic, community, and church involvement. This occurred during a designated time in the first and second services on Youth Sunday, which is the second Sunday of each month. They were presented with a Certificate of Achievement. Oftentimes, they were greeted with applause and ovations from the congregation. It was a very encouraging time for the youth and children, as well as the congregation. I led the

Youth and Children's Spotlight until 1996. Those youth are now adults serving as ushers, worship leaders, ministers, deacons, community leaders, and local entrepreneurs.

I'd be remiss if I did not mention one of our outstanding youth, Anyanna Jackson, aka Anyanna Jackson-Ba. She was an exceptionally gifted young member of our youth program at Allen Temple. She was an honor roll student during her junior and high school years in the Oakland public school system and was enrolled in AP courses at UC Berkeley in 2002. She was the premier recipient of the Youth and Children's Spotlight Award for outstanding scholarship.

Anyanna and her sister used to take the bus to the J. Alfred Smith Fellowship Hall after school to attend Pastor J. Alfred Smith, Senior's Thursday Night Bible Study at Allen Temple. I would take them home after class. After church one Sunday, she approached me with an interesting question: "Could a girl be an engineer?"

"Yes," I replied. My mental wheels started turning, and I connected her to one of our Allen Temple members, a young woman who, at the time, worked at NASA as an engineer. They met, and she encouraged Anyanna to follow her dreams. After graduating from high school with honors, Anyanna was accepted into California State Polytechnic University, Pomona, College of Engineering.

She graduated in 2008 with a Bachelor of Science degree in engineering.

The historic Allen Temple Baptist Church's legacy of biblically based preaching, teaching, and training continues today under the dynamic leadership of Reverend Doctor Jacqueline A. Thompson, who has served as senior pastor since 2017. I'm honored and blessed to serve under her leadership as a member of the Public Ministry Committee led by Sister Allie Whitehurst.

Today, Marcus "Goody" Goodloe, Ph.D. is the author of several books and continues his mission of mentoring young people, athletes, business professionals, faith-based community leaders, educators, and entertainers on issues of faith, interpersonal relationships, team synergy, character formation, and cultural relationships.

THE FAITH-BASED OAKLAND COALITION OF CONGREGATIONS

During my three years as president of the Oakland Coali-tion of Congregations, (OCC) which consisted of 17 faith-based congregations and one community organiza-tion, I had many discussions and with the training and support of Mary Gonzales of the Gamaliel Foundation carried out actions (a form of protests) with laypeople and clergy alike to fulfill our duty to serve and supply the needs of people in the East Oakland communities and beyond.

In 2001, Allen Temple Missionary Baptist Church asked me to represent the church as a member of the Oakland Coalition of Congregations. A year later, then-president Linda Handy's term expired, and I was elected president and chairman of the board for a two-year term. At the end of my two-year term, the board voted to extend my service for an additional year, which was consistent with the organization's bylaws.

Both the OCC and Clergy Caucus boards were structured to consist of one member from each congregation, totaling 18 board members. The organization consisted of Churches – Catholic and protestant, 1 Mosque, a synagogue, and one community organization. The Clergy Caucus, to which OCC was accountable, consisted of one minister from each congregation. Each board met separately once a month.

I was fortunate to have as my vice president a passionate and dedicated woman, Sherry Larsen Baville, a long-time Oakland resident and community activist. Clifford Gilmore was the executive director of OCC. Mary Gonzalez, lead trainer for the Gamaliel National Network, rounded out the leadership team.

Our activities included training both clergy and laity to organize their congregations and neighborhoods to address specific governmental, social, and economic issues affecting their communities. Accomplishments under my leadership include organizing an Affordable Housing Task Force that prompted the Oakland City Council to adopt a commercial "linkage fee," which provided new funds for affordable housing development in Oakland.

We established an open-door policy to facilitate continuous dialogue with Mayor Jerry Brown and Police Chief Richard Word, addressing issues of public safety and the lack of economic investment in East Oakland. We led the effort to ensure that local minority contractors obtained their fair share of construction contracts in the Oakland International Airport expansion project. OCC also helped gather signatures from Oakland voters to put the Just Cause Eviction Initiative on the November ballot and worked diligently to ensure a high voter turnout. The initiative, Measure EE, was approved by Oakland voters in 2002.

Please note that Just Cause Eviction is not to be confused with the COVID-19 Moratorium on Evictions established by cities and counties in 2020 that infuriated local landlords and homeowners attempting to sell their tenant-occupied properties. Under the COVID-19 Eviction Moratorium, tenants could not be evicted for as long as the moratorium was in effect, which could only be lifted by city and county mandates.

During the COVID-19 Pandemic, some cities lifted the moratorium only to have the county intervene, thereby extending moratoriums and prohibiting evictions of tenants, even if they were not paying rent. The moratorium frustrated property owners and real estate agents alike, causing devastating financial losses to thousands of Oakland property owners.

The Just Cause Eviction Ordinance, on the other hand, is a permanent legal change enacted by the California state Legislature. It is a form of tenant protection that prohibits a landlord from evicting a tenant without just cause when the tenant is in good standing and has resided in the property for at least a year. The purpose of the law is to promote housing stability through legislation.

During my tenure as president, we added three new congregations to OCC: The Islamic Cultural Center of Northern California, Taylor Memorial United Methodist Church, and St. Paul Lutheran Church. This brought the total number of congregations to 18, representing over 4,000 members, which included one community organization. At the end of my term, the board of directors presented me with the Board Leadership Award. For that, I am grateful.

Faith-based institutions like OCC, OCO, Pastors of Oakland, Faith in Action, and others serve as models for how interfaith congregations can collaborate to achieve great things for the communities they represent.

They are beacons of hope for those residents in Oakland communities who lack access to the civic apparatus and political power structure that governs their basic livelihood.

Chapter 7
Embracing The Future

Taking action is the most important first step toward success. The world doesn't pay you for what you know; It pays you for what you do.

— Jack Canfield

EMBRACING THE TECHNOLOGY OF THE FUTURE

Coming out of computer programming in the Information Technology world, I found the real estate sector in the 1990s to be way behind the times. I struggled with the antiquated MLS system. Adjusting was challenging. The minimal use of technology, even in the early 1990s, hindered the growth and efficiency of the real estate industry as a whole. Processing handwritten paper contracts was time-consuming and cumbersome.

Manually processing the paperwork associated with a transaction is a time-consuming process. Most buyers and sellers got the information they needed from agents, print advertising, and word of mouth. When I first started working as an agent, the typical office was equipped with an antiquated desktop computer, a black-and-white copier, and a fax machine.

Each agent was assigned a desk, a landline telephone, a local telephone phone book, and a catalog of black-and-white photos of the front of the house. It listed the active, pending, and sold properties. Cold calling, door-knocking, and direct mail were the primary lead-generation activities for real estate agents. Office staff and human resources were equally challenged.

The growing use of personal computers, email communications, and personal websites was the beginning of the technological evolution in the real estate industry in the late 1990s and early 2000s.

Over the past 20 years, I've witnessed firsthand the evolution of technology in the real estate sector. Today, to say the real estate industry has embraced technology is an understatement. The use of big data analytics and mobile devices has transformed the real estate industry into a data-driven marketing powerhouse for brokerages and their agents, providing highly efficient services to consumers. Real estate technology has erased geographical boundaries for home searches and exponentially extended service areas for agents.

THE POWER OF THE INTERNET

Realtor.com came on the real estate scene in 1995 as the Realtor Information Network. By 2004, the Multiple Listing Service (MLS) began to give way to digital platforms with the entry of Redfin into the market. Trulia, the San Francisco-based company, was followed in 2005 by Zillow, LinkedIn, Facebook, Instagram, and TikTok. These platforms enable consumers, homebuyers, and sellers to search for and view homes, as well as conduct comparison shopping, anywhere in the world, right from their kitchen table.

Technology has profoundly transformed the real estate industry, from agents' marketing strategies to the way properties are viewed, purchased, managed, and sold. Danny Kattan, a Forbes Council member, sums it up this way: "Virtual tours, online listings, data analytics, smart home technology, and blockchain are a few examples of how technology has reshaped the landscape of real estate."

Add to his list social media, video conferencing, messaging apps, artificial intelligence, augmented reality, and you'll get the big picture of the transformation taking place in the real estate sector today. Messaging apps provide real-time communication between buyers, sellers, real estate professionals, and all related service providers involved in a transaction.

Physical property listings on digital platforms was a paradigm shift that empowered real estate professionals and consumers with new possibilities and opportunities to search for homes, market properties for sale, attract new clients, and provide superior service to clients across geographical boundaries.

SERVING CLIENTS IN THE DIGITAL AGE

Real estate technology tools are transforming the way agents work with buyers and sellers. Using artificial intelligence, users can apply big data analytics to analyze vast amounts of market data, more precisely analyze property values, and create unique marketing strategies. Virtual reality enables an agent to showcase a property to a buyer through a headset.

The headset allows a buyer to view the property as if they were physically walking through it. For properties with upside potential where certain renovations are planned but not yet completed, the agent can use augmented reality to overlay relevant portions of the property, showing a buyer the property's potential upside without requiring an in-person visit. Awareness and mastery of real estate technology that's reshaping the future of real estate sales and service are vital to agents' success.

Real estate technology tools can make professionals more efficient and accurate, providing better service to our clients. It's important to note here that the NAR report stated that while "97 percent of buyers and sellers are searching for homes online, real estate agents continue to play a critical role in the home buying and selling process." The value that an agent brings to the transaction in terms of first-hand knowledge and experience of a particular neighborhood, local customs and values that could affect property values, the goodwill associated with the area of interest, and plans for the area before the plans become public knowledge cannot be duplicated by AI, not yet.

This chapter aims to provide you with a glimpse into the current application of artificial intelligence in the real estate sector today. This is not intended to be an exhaustive list of platforms and applications where consumers and agents utilize AI in the real estate sector. Technology touches our lives in obvious ways: smartphones, Siri, GPS, QR codes, and in ways we aren't aware of. ChatGPT and Copilot are becoming commonplace among savvy consumers. This chapter serves as an introduction to some of these tools, designed to make our lives easier, more productive, and help us take advantage of new opportunities when used for the common good.

A PARADIGM SHIFT

Physical property listing on digital platforms was a paradigm shift that empowered real estate professionals and consumers with new possibilities and opportunities to search for homes, market properties for sale, attract new clients, and provide superior service to clients across geographical boundaries.

According to a 2021 survey from the National Association of Realtors (NAR), nearly 97% of homebuyers begin their search for a home online. The percentage of home buyers using the internet to search for homes in 1995 was 2 percent. In 2019, NAR reported that over 80 percent of millennials used a mobile device to find their home. I venture to say that number is considerably higher today.

Artificial intelligence enables faster and more accurate property searches during real estate transactions. Typically, a title search in a real estate transaction can take anywhere from a few hours to between 7 and 14 days, depending on the property's history. This timeframe is based on my own experience working with title companies that process real estate transactions.

The process of a title search is to confirm the rightful owner and verify whether the property is free from encumbrances, and to ensure there is no break in the "chain of title" from the time the home was first sold until the current sale. Some properties will have been sold multiple times in a given period, while others may have sold only once in 30, 40, or 50 years. It's a painstaking, mostly manual process that's carried out for each property sale. Paper records require more time and effort to manage.

Artificial Intelligence has accelerated the paperless age, where records are digitized, organized, and stored for easy retrieval during title searches. Using AI, retrieval time is reduced from days to minutes. And get this: according to my research, the customer experience can also be "enabled and automated" through online customer portals. AI can capture a buyer's or a seller's data and preferences, thereby providing personalized service in the future.

The power of AI lies in its ability to process massive amounts of data in seconds, which enables it to analyze extensive market datasets to identify trends that can predict human behavior and demographics, and provide marketing strategies related to a prospective seller's intentions and timing for entering the real estate market. Through prompting, agents are utilizing AI to accurately calculate property values, generate content, develop a winning social media strategy, and create auto-responses to voluminous inquiries, thereby freeing up the agent's time to focus on direct service to clients and lead generation.

Artificial intelligence is a potent tool that's changing the way and the speed at which agents carry out their fiduciary duties and responsibilities to their clients. Powerful though it may be at analyzing human behavior, it will not replace the human element that a live, breathing professional can provide. The real estate agent will remain indispensable. AI is another tool that frees up the agent's valuable time, improves accuracy, and efficiency. It can also detect fraudulent documents more easily than human observation. This helps the agent provide more accurate and timely service.

The following are some of the ways Artificial Intelligence is currently being used in real estate today. This is a partial list to raise awareness. This list is not intended to be comprehensive of all Artificial Intelligence applications in today's real estate environment. This is just the tip of the iceberg. AI will not replace real estate agents. However, agents who do not use AI will be replaced by those who do.

Predictive Analysis. Using algorithms (a set of rules and instructions) and analyzing vast amounts of data, AI can accurately predict market trends and property values more efficiently than traditional methods used by agents.

Property condition assessment. AI is currently being used to automate the evaluation of a property's condition, analyzing MLS data, MLS photos, and individual features to evaluate the overall quality of the property, leading to more accurate property valuation.

Customer Service. Powered by chatbots (utilizing a simulated human voice), customer service is available 24 hours a day, 7 days a week. AI provides instant responses to inquiries, instant access to information, answers common questions, schedules interviews, sets appointments, and offers property recommendations.

Client behavior. AI can analyze client interactions and preferences to identify trends and tailor future interactions accordingly. AI can predict a client's future actions by processing massivet datasets from diverse data sources to identify trends and patterns, thereby gaining a deeper understanding of their preferences. Using this information, it can then predict future actions and personalize future interactions with the client.

Risk Management. AI can analyze and process massive amounts of data to identify patterns of anomalies and predict potential threats that human analysis might miss. Ultimately, AI improves efficiency and accuracy in the risk management process.

Mortgage underwriting. AI is transforming mortgage underwriting by analyzing vast amounts of data (one of AI's most powerful tools) to gain a more comprehensive view of a borrower's creditworthiness. It can also explore a borrower's data, credit history, and other factors to assess risk and determine loan eligibility, streamlining the entire underwriting process. AI can adapt underwriting criteria to changing market conditions and buyers' profiles. This all ensures the underwriting process remains relevant and practical.

DISPELLING THE MYTH THAT COACHES PREY ON AGENTS' FEARS AND INSECURITIES

Coaching, like any other business, has its doubters and detractors. Some of the negative comments about coaching include: "They (coaches) prey on our fears and insecurities," "Most have never sold a house in their lives." "Many coaches don't have adequate experience." "I'm better than the coach I hired." "It (coaching) became repetitive and predictable once the fundamentals were learned." Others cited the cost as a factor in not hiring a coach. And on and on.

WE WERE COACHED LONG BEFORE WE BECAME "EXPERTS"

Practically everything we learned in the early years of our lives, we learned through coaching. Our coaches were our parents, our teachers, and family friends. Class-rooms introduced us to the necessary subjects and activities we needed to stay safe, live healthy, and grow in the knowledge we needed to achieve academic success.

We were held accountable for doing homework and completing assignments on time. Then we left home, went to institutions of higher learning, and abandoned the idea of coaching. We were free! We were glad to get away from controlling parents, teachers, and counselors.

Perhaps it's time to rethink the way you think about coaching. Research shows that coaching can transform you and your career to achieve greater success. I contend that if we want to continue growing in knowledge and expertise in our personal and professional lives, we need a coach. Coaching will get you out of your comfort zone and into your opportunity zone.

Outside of our comfort zone is the only place where real growth takes place. Remarkably, successful people don't seek comfort. They strive for success beyond their comfort zone. In doing so, they get comfortable being uncomfortable. And therein lies the key to achieving great success. Having a coach is not a universal necessity. But every very highly successful person has a coach. Case in point: Warren Buffett, Barack Obama, Oprah Winfrey, Serena Williams, the late Steve Jobs, and the famous musical group Metallica all have coaches or have had coaches in the past.

COACHING HAS MANY POSITIVE BENEFITS

The results of an Inman *Special report, "Real Estate Coaching Payoff,"* showed that 80% of real estate agents cited being "held accountable" as the most significant benefit of working with a coach, according to the Inman survey. 77% said their coach "provides perspective", and 76% cited "training them to use certain business strategies" as a benefit. Others noted a real estate coach "let me know what others are doing to be successful so I don't have to reinvent the wheel." Another agent reported, "They (coaches) help me see things clearly, help me focus, [and] put things into perspective."

REAL ESTATE COACHING PAYS OFF

The 2015 Inman survey was the most comprehensive report I found detailing the value of coaching. One of the questions was "How much did your business increase during the first year you worked with a coach compared to the previous year?" Of the **988** respondents, 35% reported that their business increased by 10% to 25%. Nearly 20% said their business increased between 26% and 49%. Fifteen percent of respondents reported increases between 100% and 199%.

Another agent reported, "Coaches help me see things clearly and help me focus, and put things into perspective, and are an unbiased second eye.

"Even with 20 years of experience, I still need someone to help keep me motivated and on task. I like one-on-one attention. I don't get that from my manager," commented another.

What do all highly successful people have in common? They have coaches. Coaches are *knowledge brokers* and results-oriented collaborators who can help you discover powerful new insights and step into a new chapter of success.

THE DIFFERENT WAYS A COACH CAN IMPROVE YOUR BUSINESS

Goal Setting: Unleashing the power of goal setting is one of the crucial success principles. A coach will help you set clear goals, hold you accountable, and improve self-management techniques. You decide what goal you want to reach and within what timeframe. A coach can also help bridge the gap between the goals you set and the actions you take to achieve those goals. Keeping you on track and on time is vital to your success.

Strategizing: A coach helps you navigate and overcome challenges, boosting your self-awareness so you can discover your untapped potential. A great strategy can outperform experience. Your coach can also help you leverage technology, brainstorm the best products and platforms for your needs, and integrate them into your workflow for optimal results.

Minimizing weaknesses: It's challenging for most of us to accurately assess our abilities, especially when we fall short. A coach can help you identify areas for improvement. More importantly, if working on your challenges takes too much time and energy, a coach will train you how to play to your strengths. People who invest their energy in developing their strengths instead of correcting their deficiencies have more potential for exponential growth. Remember, you can always hire someone to do the things that challenge your abilities.

Staying focused: A good coach will help on the most crucial asks. What you focus on expands. The most important tasks are those you can accomplish that will make the remaining tasks easier or unnecessary.

A coach not only helps you set goals and figure out how to achieve them, but also enables you to maintain your commitment and determine whether your current performance will produce the outcome you set as your end goal. A coach will hold you accountable and keep your performance on track to reach your goal within the allotted time. I use time blocking to help me stay focused on the most critical tasks. Time blocking is a time management strategy where I divide my day into designated blocks of time for specific tasks.

Evaluating your performance: Without feedback, it is nearly impossible to improve your performance. Using feedback, we can both determine whether you're on track to achieve your goal. You will move further and faster by taking action on the feedback you receive from your coach. You'll receive data, advice, help, suggestions, and direction. A coach will provide honest and constructive feedback, which sometimes can be hard to swallow, but can be crucial for you to grow into a top-producing agent. A coach can also help you make necessary adjustments to stay on track toward your goal. I encourage you to *ask* for feedback whenever you need it.

IDENTIFYING MISSING SKILLS

A coach will provide you with a mental edge that could take you months to discover on your own. For the real estate agent, a coach will assess your ongoing list of tasks and help you figure out what skills you may be missing. A coach can prevent issues from arising and help you maintain a seamless experience for your client.

A Broader Perspective: Finally, a coach can broaden your perspective through increased self-awareness, which can help you discover the core genius you may not be able to identify on your own. Even if you're a brilliant entrepreneur, you can't always see your blind spots.

As a coach, I work with top leaders from diverse professions and demographics across a wide variety of market areas. I learn from my clients and can share their successes and failures, their stories, and A-Ha moments with you, which you wouldn't otherwise discover. Again, success leaves clues.

The coaching methods I use to produce outstanding outcomes include creating a comfortable physical and mental space for expression, providing clear instructions for learning and sharing, modeling mastery and authenticity, and relate to the main learning styles: auditory, kinesthetic, and visual, open-minded, transparent, compassionate, mindful, and creative. The focus here is on engaging and connecting on a deep level with the client. And finally, great coaching requires establishing clear guidelines and expectations for learning. Great coaches also share entertaining and relevant stories to make key points and provide knowledge as the expert in the room.

WHAT TO LOOK FOR IN A COACH

When working with a coach, look for the following: experience, knowledge of the subject matter, track record of success, accomplishments, recommendations, testimonials, compatibility, coaching style (drill sergeant, cheerleader, coach/player), coaching philosophy, honesty, integrity, compassion, accountability, pleasant attitude, patient, mindful, return on investment.

CALL TO ACTION

Nothing happens until something moves. If you want to know why you're not where you want to be in life today, it's because you have beliefs that are holding you back. Have you ever backed out of your driveway without releasing the parking brake? I sure have. As I started down the street, I could feel something holding the car back from gaining speed. Then, I realized the parking brake was on. Now, I have two choices: I can ignore the parking brake and press harder on the accelerator to gain speed, or I can release the brake.

What I discovered when I was going through the furnace of limiting beliefs, self-doubt, negative self-talk, and holding on to old negative beliefs is like driving through life with your parking brake on. Our beliefs control us. The way we process our past experiences and what we believe to be true when we feel stuck or face tough new challenges will determine the outcome. To change my circumstances, I had to interrupt the pattern of thoughts I was thinking and the erroneous beliefs I was holding onto.

I utilized self-awareness, intuition, faith, and positive affirmations to shift my mindset from limiting beliefs and negative thinking to positive thoughts. This helped me regain my true beliefs. This *shift* allowed me to develop new behaviors, new habits, and a new self-image that aligned with my values and the person I aspired to be. This process was not easy, and it didn't happen overnight. The key to successfully overcoming adversity when you're feeling stuck and overwhelmed is to take one small positive action step at a time. Start today. Start *now*.

If you find yourself struggling to restore hope and find your way out of a difficult situation, ask yourself:

What's the *one small step* you can take today that will shift the pattern of negative thoughts and beliefs that's holding you back? Embracing positive thoughts and beliefs will lift you up and take you from where you are now to where you intend to be in the future.

ABOUT AIM HIGH COACHING

If you're ready to step into a new chapter of your success, please reach out to start a conversation. Nothing happens until something moves. Ultimately, you must take action. My door is open. Feel free to take advantage of my "Ask me any questions, no-obligation, 30-minute coaching session."

About Aim Coaching

Aim High Coaching is a coaching and training business. My mission is to partner with clients in a thought-provoking and creative process that empowers you to discover your inner strength, enabling you to create the success, freedom, and quality of life they desire by applying *The Success Principles* in nine key areas of your life. We dive deeply into each of these key areas in our workshops.

As a Canfield Certified Trainer and Coach, I utilize the proven, time-tested systems of *The Success Principles,* which produce transformational growth and development in the lives of those I have the privilege of training and coaching.

Aim High Coaching offers this training in half-day workshops, multiple-day workshops, group coaching, one-on-one coaching, and transformational speaking engagements. This program is offered online and in person. Our clients include athletes, entrepreneurs, executives, real estate agents, and everyday individuals who seek to enhance their self-awareness and achieve peak performance in all aspects of their lives.

MORAL OF THE STORY

Our beliefs control all aspects of our personal and professional lives. To be highly successful, we must set big goals and believe that reaching our goal is possible. Never let your current circumstances dictate your future. We're greater than our circumstances. Believe in a higher power, then take action. Remember, scripture reminds us that faith without works is dead.

"I am victorious" must be your battle cry when self-doubt invades your consciousness. Stay focused. Keep your eyes on the prize – your goal, your big Why. You must maintain a mindset that you are worthy of success! You have value. Your purpose-driven life creates the kind of success that results in significance. It is in significance that we find joy.

Success and happiness based on skills, techniques, behavior, social image, fame and money can be fleeting, leaving you to answer the question, "Is this all there is?" In order to achieve true happiness, your success must align with your values – values like service, integrity, patience, fidelity, justice, and the golden rule. Then you will find happiness, significance, fulfillment, and ultimately, joy.

Joy is the fruit of our labor found in helping others achieve more than they ever thought possible. This is the joy that the world didn't give you, and the world can't take it away.

Acknowledgments

Special thanks to my friend Elaine Lee, who referred me to the talented and empathetic editor, Amberly Finarelli. Amberly's insightful feedback kept me focused and gave form to the narrative for this book. She invested her time, heart, and energy into providing structure to my streams of conscientiousness early on. A special portion of gratitude goes to Harold Pendergrass, Otis Bruce, Jonathan Fleming, and Joel Freid for their unwavering support through the years. Many thanks to Charlotte E. Saulter, owner and administrator at CES Real Estate School, for hiring me to teach prelicensing real estate courses to her students. Thanks also go out to Melenda Cohan and team at The Coaches Console.

I also want to thank the following individuals: Nia Shakur, my part-time assistant since 2014, who has been the behind-the-scenes go-to person supporting me in my real estate and coaching business. Her moral and technical support over the years has helped me stay in the game. Thanks also go to Lawrence Benford, who fact-checked crucial portions of my manuscript, and Travis Benford, whose keen recall of details provided accuracy for some of my personal stories.

Special thanks to Don Askey, my friend and "accountability partner" who keeps me focused and encouraged when I can't see the light at the end of the tunnel; Melvin Benford for sharing stories about our Little League and Pony League baseball teams, from which I gleaned some of the facts included in this book; Ira Newsome for his recall of names, dates, and statistics for our Little League and Pony League teams; Eddie Walker, retired real estate broker, who every Sunday after church would ask me, "How's that book coming?" I also want to thank my sister Madelyn, who encouraged me to expand my thinking and keep an open mind about the title for my book.

I'm so grateful for my coaches and trainers who, during my career, provided the structure and methodologies that formed the foundation for my success: Ollie Fleet, Fae Bidgoli, Craig Proctor, Nate Brooks, Tom Ziglar, Jack Canfield, Lisa Nichols, Gary Keller, Tena Jones, Tim & Julie Harris, and Patrice Washington.

I am especially grateful for my high school teacher, Mrs.Gladys Hogan, who taught English and Literature. Her expectations for mastery of English and exegesis of a topic inspire me to this day. I'm deeply indebted to Mrs. Maggie Simpson, my fourth through eighth-grade teacher and principal, who provided me with an expansive curriculum unique to my seemingly insatiable appetite for reading and learning.

I acknowledge Reverend Charlotte Myers, who shared her ideas and prayers, and encouraged me from the beginning to keep writing until the book was done. It's done, Charlotte. Thank you. A big shout-out to Melissa G. Wilson at Networlding Publishing. This collaborative-minded publisher's authenticity and values align with the purpose of this book and my future goals. Melissa has been a godsend for this book's success.

And, of course, where would I be without God on my side? The Reverend Dr. Jacqueline A. Thompson, my pastor, and Reverend Dr. J. Alfred Smith, Sr., my Pastor Emeritus at Allen Temple Baptist Church in Oakland, keep me spiritually grounded and walking by faith. I'd be remiss if I did not give a heartfelt expression of gratitude to Reverend Gary W. Jones, the current pastor of Allwise Missionary Baptist Church in Chappell Hill, Texas, for his outstanding leadership in the church and the community at large. This was the church of my parents. This is where I confessed my faith in Christ. Reverend Jones led the celebration of the church's 150th anniversary in 2024.

I owe a debt of gratitude to my parents, who taught me to read, write, and pray; to speak clearly and avoid talking "foolishness." If they were still here today, they would be my biggest promoters for this book. My dad would be on the telephone, calling everybody he knew, telling them, "Roy Lee just wrote a book!" I can hear my dad now saying, "Here, you can have my copy; I'll get another one from him." Thank you both from the bottom of my heart. May you rest in the glory of heavenly peace.

Step Into a New Chapter of Success

Whether leading keynote presentations, hosting group trainings, or coaching one-on-one, Roy uses *The Success Principles* as his guide to move his audience from where they are to where they want to be. His signature coaching program *Mastering The Core Principles of Success* is rooted in principle number one: Take 100% Responsibility for Your Life.

Roy's influence also extends to public speaking. He's a sought-after speaker, guest lecturer, and master of ceremonies, known for his ability to connect deeply with his audiences. His partnerships include Merritt College, the National Association of Real Estate Brokers, and CES Real Estate School. His insights have been featured in the Oakland Post and Marin Independent Journal.

Connect with Roy at www.aimhighcoaching.com

Before You Go

Before you go, I'd like to request a bit more of your time. If you found this book helpful, I would be so grateful if you would please leave a short review on Amazon.

Even if you read only one or two chapters, you could mention why those insights helped you on your consulting journey or something you might avoid doing in the future. Books like this are buried in a sea of books unless kind, generous readers like you take the time to post honest reviews. When reviews are posted, the algorithms take note and promote the book to other potential readers.

Thank you in advance for this generous expression of your appreciation. Your review will encourage me to spend more time sharing my advice with the public in this way. Being able to help others through writing means everything to me.

You can also email me directly with your thoughts at **roy.benford@gmail.com**. I'd love to hear from you.

www.ingramcontent.com/pod-product-compliance
Lightning Source LLC
Chambersburg PA
CBHW061745120626
46550CB00005B/1894